T0128164

Reclaiming
Purity

*My Journey to Live God's Way in a Christian
Dating Relationship, and in Marriage*

LAURA C. MAYER

WESTBOW
PRESS®
A DIVISION OF THOMAS NELSON
& ZONDERVAN

Copyright © 2018 Laura C. Mayer.

All rights reserved. No part of this book may be used or reproduced by
any means, graphic, electronic, or mechanical, including photocopying,
recording, taping or by any information storage retrieval system
without the written permission of the author except in the case of
brief quotations embodied in critical articles and reviews.

This book is a work of non-fiction. Unless otherwise noted, the author
and the publisher make no explicit guarantees as to the accuracy of
the information contained in this book and in some cases, names
of people and places have been altered to protect their privacy.

THE HOLY BIBLE, NEW INTERNATIONAL VERSION®,
NIV® Copyright © 1973, 1978, 1984, 2011 by Biblica, Inc.®
Used by permission. All rights reserved worldwide.

WestBow Press books may be ordered through booksellers or by contacting:

WestBow Press
A Division of Thomas Nelson & Zondervan
1663 Liberty Drive
Bloomington, IN 47403
www.westbowpress.com
1 (866) 928-1240

Because of the dynamic nature of the Internet, any web addresses or
links contained in this book may have changed since publication and
may no longer be valid. The views expressed in this work are solely those
of the author and do not necessarily reflect the views of the publisher,
and the publisher hereby disclaims any responsibility for them.

Any people depicted in stock imagery provided by Getty Images are
models, and such images are being used for illustrative purposes only.
Certain stock imagery © Getty Images.

ISBN: 978-1-9736-4527-6 (sc)
ISBN: 978-1-9736-4528-3 (hc)
ISBN: 978-1-9736-4526-9 (e)

Library of Congress Control Number: 2018913484

Print information available on the last page.

WestBow Press rev. date: 08/21/2019

Contents

Introduction

"So I find this law at work; when I want to do good, evil is right there with me. For in my inner being I delight in God's law; but I see another law at work in the members of my body, waging war against the law of my mind and making me a prisoner of the law of sin at work within my members. What a wretched man I am! Who will save me from this body of death? Thanks be to God—through Jesus Christ our Lord!" Romans 7:21-25

I was torn. I felt God's conviction cautioning me to stop. But deep within me was a longing for this boy to hold me—to gaze into my eyes and tell me I was beautiful and desirable...to reassure me just one more time. Kissing him was inviting escalating passion as I felt him respond to me. But I didn't want to go too far. How far was too far? Can you relate to this struggle?

The Bible is very clear that sex before marriage is outside of God's plan for His people. Hebrews 13:4 says, *"Marriage should be honored by all, and the marriage bed kept pure, for God will judge the adulterer and all the sexually immoral."* I am not just trying to convince you to seek purity before marriage. If you have picked up this book, I assume you have already made the commitment to purity, or at least you feel that quiet conviction that I did in my dating years. But maybe you, too, struggle with how to implement it. As the verse in Romans 7 above suggests, the problem is not just a lack of knowledge of God's standards; it's the difficulty in resisting the temptation to violate them. Paul says that even though He loves God's law and wants to do good, evil is right there with him. There's a tension between what our spirit knows to be right and the pull of our flesh. So once we make a commitment to purity, what happens next?

It took Brian, my husband, and me some time to grasp the idea of purity while we were dating. After reading our story, you'll see that making the commitment to purity was just the beginning. We had tasted the forbidden fruit for a number of years. Then I got to know Jesus in a new and powerful way. Brian eventually followed and we knew things had to change. We had the difficult task of trying to figure out how to have a Christian dating relationship, living in the Garden of Eden so to speak, right next to the tree but resisting the habit and compulsion of reaching for that fruit. How close to the forbidden tree can you get? Can you actually hold the apple in your hand but not taste it? There is no hard and fast rule I can give you for where to draw the line. However, I will share with you some lessons that I learned to show you how to build your relationship together through Christian dating. I will describe some strategies to keep the pilot light of your passion lit but under God's gentle control. Then, how does it work to take two imperfect people, joined under God to become one in a loving marriage?

I want to give you some ideas for ways to invest time in your relationship that won't rob you of your purity but will help you to explore one another in new ways—to develop the emotional, intellectual and, most of all, spiritual sides of your relationship together. You may or may not be 100% sure of your future together. That's ok. I believe God will provide clarity. In any case, you're not just dating to pass the time. You're dating with a purpose: to see if you're compatible together. If you keep God in the center of your relationship, rather than just a passing thought on Sunday, He will bless your lives abundantly. He will guide you in the way you should go, and if it is His plan to join you in marriage one day, He will honor your vows of purity and help you grow and change in a blossoming relationship.

.

One

Our Story

"I am the Lord your God, who teaches you what is best for you, who directs you in the way you should go." Isaiah 48:17

There was something mysterious about Brian that drew me to him. I wanted to crack him open and learn all his secrets. He was a good listener, had a positive personality, made funny jokes, and wrote poetry. He didn't seem to care what people thought of him. I felt that he was someone I could have a relationship with on a deeper level.

We caught each other's eye in chemistry class and slowly got acquainted for several months through a history class during our junior year of high school together. One day, he walked up to my locker as I was gathering my books. My heart was pounding. I hoped he was intending to ask for my phone number. Why else would a boy approach a girl's locker in high school? Instead, he said, "Hey, do you remember Jackson? He

wanted me to ask you for your number." I hoped he could see
the disappointment in my face. Jackson was a friend of his.
He had actually been my boyfriend during freshman year, but
had since moved to another high school. Apparently the two of
them had been talking about me.

"Sure," I replied. At least Brian would have my number
as well. I did get a call from Jackson. He was pleasant and
we caught up in conversation. However, the puppy dog love I
previously had for him had since passed, and I got off the phone
with a feeling of closure. I did have a few other relationships
since Jackson. Some were stronger than others. I was always
timid at first, waiting weeks to hold hands, and months for a first
kiss. Never did I undress or allow wandering hands to explore
my body. It didn't feel right, and, quite honestly, I was insecure
about my small size. But I began to learn the power I could
have over a boy. I could make him yearn for me, and I learned
how to keep him wanting.

Prior to my senior year, Brian and I both went on a school
trip out West called "Summer Field Studies." We found a few
moments to talk before the vans headed out. It was a friendly
conversation, and he disclosed that he had recently broken up
with his girlfriend. I knew that now was my chance to drop a
hint. "Our timing is never right," I replied. I told him how I
had recently, just weeks before, started dating Kevin. I had met
him at a country line dancing club the very night I broke up
with Conner, when I realized that I wasn't actually in love with
him. I hadn't wanted to jump into this new relationship, but
Kevin had been persistent, and finally I agreed to date him. So
now I was spoken for.

Brian picked up on my hint and shot me a surprised look.
Months later, he described that moment as the first time he
had hope that I could be interested in him. He began to put

his efforts towards pursuing me, even though I was technically not available.

We were the only ones awake (besides the driver, luckily) in a 15 passenger van in Kansas in the middle of the night, and we just couldn't stop talking. I felt safe with him and was attracted to him. I fell asleep on his shoulder. He actually wrote a poem about that moment. But as the trip progressed, he began following me around like a love-struck schoolboy. I started to regret opening up to him and luring him emotionally in this way. After all, I *was* still dating Kevin, and had just broken Conner's heart. Months before that was Matt and prior to him, Jackson. I knew it wasn't right to jump from relationship to relationship. Was I being too hasty with Brian? Was he really so different than the others, or was I going to break his heart as well? I had to stop him before it got too involved. I told him, "I'm sorry, but I *am* in a relationship right now. I like you, but I can't start dating you until I get home and decide if I'm going to stay with Kevin or not." Brian backed off, but I had already told him in the middle of the night in that van that I wasn't in love with Kevin. So he didn't lose hope, but saw this as merely a setback. I felt his eyes at my back as I tried to ignore him, while we hiked the most beautiful hike of my life in the Grand Canyon.

I had a chance to call Kevin from out West. His parents were gone on vacation, and he bragged to me about the party he had in their absence. Beer was involved, and he laughed about a girl passing out in his bedroom. Kevin was a sweet guy, but he was easily influenced by his cousins who, shall we say, didn't make the best moral decisions. I just knew as I got off the phone with him that it wasn't going to work out. I was not a drinker, or a partier, and I was trying to keep some boundaries in place physically. I *wanted* to do what was right. Kevin wanted what we all want… to be accepted by others and liked. When I got home from Summer Field Studies, I ended our month-long relationship amidst his tears.

Later that summer, after some encouragement from my mom and sister Amy, I decided to call Brian. They thought I was crazy for letting him go, after I described the late night talks and the poetry and notes he gave me. Maybe they were right and I shouldn't let this one pass me by. But was it too late? Would he still be hurt that I turned him down in Arizona? I dialed his number. He answered the phone and seemed happy to hear from me. I told Brian that I did break up with Kevin, and had been thinking of him since the trip. We went on our first date to Dairy Queen, with my hair perfectly curled and makeup done with precision. Then I got to meet his entire family on the 4th of July during a cookout at his dad's house. It was innocent enough. We tossed a Frisbee, and he caught his shirt on fire. No injuries. But there were definitely fireworks going off in my heart, as I wondered if this boy really liked me.

Believe it or not, we had both also signed up for an Appalachian mission trip later that same summer. During this time, we began dating officially and were joined at the hip. We dug out earth behind a home nestled next to an eroding mountainside. I noticed his strong build and contagious smile. We painted rooms in a low income house, and hauled off trash together, locking eyes, and joking along the way. We knew we were serving people, and also serving God, and it all felt right. In a room full of sleeping people one night he told me, "Laura, if I don't love you now, it's inevitable." I melted, of course.

I smiled and replied, "Me too."

Here is an example of one of his sweet poems he wrote for me. Doesn't every girl want to hear things like this?

I lie awake.
My eyes,
Peering into the darkness.
Tick-tock, tick-tock, tick-tock.
The sound marches into my ears,
Filling them, making my mind wander
To you.
Would I sleep if you were near me? Could I?
How I long to know.
To reach out my arm and caress you.
To draw you near
Not for one fleeting moment,
But instead, for a lifetime.
To hug you and tell you
I love you,
Always and forever.
But I cannot.
So I lie awake tonight thinking of you.
And wishing you were here.

I believe we were both nominal, on the fence Christians. We were each seeking God in our own ways and times. I went to a Catholic Church every Sunday. He attended Mass occasionally with his dad. He helped everyone in need, and was forever finding people stranded on the side of the road with a flat tire. Right up front we both admitted that, while we were virgins, we had taken past relationships too far physically. We made an agreement to take things slow and save sex for marriage. Well that's easier said than done.

There were flowers and love notes and dates, which usually consisted of watching a movie in my parents' basement after dinner. I eventually got the ball rolling by kissing him first. He held back because of our mutual agreement but this made me doubtful of his love and attraction towards me. We warmed up over time and pressed forward with our physical intimacy, as well as our emotional intimacy. We kissed and cuddled and eventually our hands began exploring. As he told me over and over that I was beautiful, I began to let the ground slip that I had held so firmly before. The clothing began to come off. I was insecure, but he called me "*Gorgeous*," and the feeling that maybe I could satisfy him and be enough was tempting beyond measure. Once in a while I would try to draw a line, out of guilt. He would respect that line and, two weeks later, I wondered why he was no longer attracted to me on a physical level. I would initiate the petting sessions again, with some kind of rationalization, and the cycle would repeat. Why did I torment him so? I realize now that because my self-worth was wrapped up in my appearance, I needed to feel physically attractive and sexually desirable. I was so insecure in his love for me that I craved the physical attention from him to fulfill my emotional needs.

Well, eventually, we were doing everything but intercourse very regularly and completely justifying it. We each were able to achieve sensations I didn't know were possible. We did end up trying sex a handful of times, but it was actually painful for me, so we never finished the act. We decided to let that sleeping dog lie. Believe it or not, I was in so much denial that I was convinced we were still saving sex for marriage.

Soon our relationship was diminished to a purely physical one. Why? We didn't have many opportunities alone, so when we were alone, you can guess what we were doing. We headed off to the same college, Xavier University, two hours from home in Cincinnati, OH and had even less accountability. Our sexual appetites were insatiable and we prided ourselves with our skills. But I remember feeling empty afterward, and lonely, while lying next to him in a college dorm room. There was less talking, and I found myself wondering what he was thinking. I knew what we were doing felt good to him and he craved it. But did he want *me*? Did he really *know* me? If he really knew me, would I be enough?

When we weren't making out, we spent lots of time arguing and being irritable with each other. Even my friends and family members noticed. He was a procrastinator, while I was a perfectionist and a planner. Sometimes I would come by his dorm room and find him still asleep, completely missing one of his classes. He was always late to pick me up, or to call me. I began to notice that sometimes his stories didn't match up. He was telling me little white lies, like saying he was doing his homework, when in reality he was hanging out with some guys at the gym. He tried to impress me by telling me a better story, but when I found out he fudged the truth, I began to lose respect and trust for him. Did he think I couldn't handle the truth? Was I really that severe? At the same time, I wondered why he didn't want to spend all his free time with me. Wasn't I enough?

You see, the world's ways and answers to life are so different than what God calls us to. I was beginning to see the damage and breakdown in my relationship with Brian as I slowly (sometimes quickly) veered from God's loving standards. There are always consequences to the sins that we choose. We rarely see that at the time. The world lures us with, "Do what feels good in the moment." The Beatles sang, "All you need is love." But the love the world talks of is more like lust and romantic sentiments. What about when the going gets rough, he's not cute first thing in the morning, or we start to see each other's weaknesses? None of us is enough for those moments. We all need something greater, deeper and more secure than a feeling. That is what our God offers to us.

Two

My Secret

"Where can I go from your Spirit? Where can I flee from your presence? If I go up to the heavens, you are there; if I make my bed in the depths, you are there." Psalm 139:7-8

I had a secret of my own. I kept it from the world, but Brian was aware to a small extent. You see, I had this weird relationship with food. I mentioned that I was self-conscious about my body and found my self-worth in my appearance. My breasts were too small but my hips were too wide. And those thighs… all I saw was cellulite and fat. I was not overweight by any stretch. People actually told me I needed to *gain* weight in high school. But I was convinced that I needed to control my diet. Every adult woman I knew was dieting and warning me to fight it off and keep my figure. Every magazine at the grocery store gave the best tips on how to lose weight. I read it all. I began "watching what I ate." I counted and wrote down all my calories, to the point that I learned how many calories were in everything I ate. I could've taught a nutrition class by age 15. I weighed myself every day like a ritual, and looked in the mirror afterwards. Weighed myself…looked in the mirror. Weighed myself…looked in the mirror. Eventually I could tell simply by looking in the mirror if I had lost or gained a couple pounds. Still stepped on the scale though.

I really didn't think this was a problem in my life. My only problem was that I couldn't maintain 110 lbs. and stay in my size 5's. Freshman year of high school we watched a video about eating disorders in a health class. Strangely, I could really relate to those girls. But I didn't have textbook anorexia which would be losing 25% of my body weight. Looking back, I see that I was buying into the following lies:

1. If I ate a hamburger, or brownie, I would instantly gain 5 lbs.
2. Others could eat what they want and not gain weight. I was different.
3. If I gained weight that would be the end—I wouldn't be able to lose it.
4. If I gained weight, no one would want to date me. Therefore, I wouldn't be able to get married or have children. It was a snowball effect.
5. If I gained weight I would let everyone down, most of all myself.

All of those lies were based in FEAR, and I thought my happiness in life really did hinge on my weight. I was so focused on such an insignificant part of who I was, my weight…which really didn't need to be changed to begin with. I was useless in the Kingdom of God. I wasn't thinking about what parts of my character needed to change, or how my coping strategies needed fixed, or how my relationships could stand to improve. I called myself a Christian, but I certainly wasn't walking victoriously.

The Bible tells us that we have an enemy, the devil, who tries to ensnare us with lies.

1 Peter 5:8-9 says, "*Be alert and of sober mind. Your enemy the devil prowls around like a roaring lion looking for someone to devour. Resist him, standing firm in the faith, because you know that the family of believers throughout the world is undergoing the same kind of sufferings.*"

In John 10:10, Jesus tells His followers, "*The thief comes only to steal, and kill and destroy; I have come that they may have life, and have it to the full.*" I didn't see it at the time, but I had an enemy, and he was cunning. With these lies, he was slowly stealing my joy, and the full life that Jesus had come to give even me was slipping away.

People started to notice my strange eating habits. I brought carrots, yogurt and fruit for lunch. My fingers turned orange from all the carotene. My nail beds turned purple with decreased circulation. Eventually after I heard, "I can't believe you're eating a salad—you need to gain weight" for the 100th time, I began to think maybe I was a little off base. Maybe I wasn't as healthy as I thought I was. So I tried to allow myself to eat from my list of forbidden foods, but I still had the guilt and shame associated with eating, and my intense fear of fat. I slipped out of control that I had worked so tightly to obtain.

I began bingeing and lost my willpower to food completely. If you've never had a binge, let me give you a mental picture—it's not just a little overindulgence that we all give into on a holiday. I'd be looking at the cookies and think, "I haven't had anything for awhile; I deserve 1 or 2 cookies." Then I would have a couple more. Then, after realizing what I was doing, which was giving in, the mentality for me would change from a reward to a punishment. Knowing how horrible it would make me feel, I'd finish off half the box, stuffing myself beyond full to the point I'd be praying to God to let me throw it up because I felt physically sick. But I wasn't ever able to carry that out… except once. So I knew I didn't have bulimia. I was thick into denial.

The binges grew closer and closer together, up to several times a day and only behind closed doors. I dieted in the open. I woke up every morning with a heavy cloud of guilt and shame, disgusted with myself for what I'd done the day before. Are we noticing a focus on self here? I thought about food all the time…either what I wanted to eat but couldn't, or what I'd eaten that I shouldn't have. Exercise was more important than ever now, to burn off the latest binge or meal

One of my lows was on the way home from visiting my sister in college at Indiana University in Bloomington, Indiana. I was proud of myself for eating pretty well all day. That was my measure. As I started my hour long trip back to Indianapolis, thoughts of food began taunting me. I decided to stop, just to get a snack for the drive home. I stopped at a gas station and opted for what I told myself was a healthier choice, a blueberry muffin loaf, not making any eye contact with the cashier for fear she'd know what I was up to. Of course I had to speed up a little once back on the road since I'd called my mom when I left and she knew what time to expect me… couldn't have her suspecting anything. I inhaled the muffin loaf before I could change my mind. But that wasn't really what I wanted and I couldn't get food out of my mind. I decided it would be best if I just got what I really wanted and got it over with so I stopped again, this time choosing a sinful candy-bar. I knew every eye was looking right through me at the gas station. Sped up a little more. Inhaled the candy bar…wasn't what I wanted. I think the next stop I actually got gas. I was so jittery from the sugar rush and the nervousness, shame and guilt I had dropped my wallet and couldn't find it as I searched through my car. Had I left it at the last gas station? How could I go back? How could I explain it to Mom? I was panicked… then I found it right on the pavement outside the car. I went inside to buy something to eat. I ended up stopping a total of five times between Bloomington and Indy with the last stop being 5 minutes from the house. My heart was racing as I walked in the door; I was late but somehow Mom didn't notice. I probably had ingested 2000 calories just on the way home. I was disgusted with myself. That, I'm sure you know, is not normal.

Well, eventually I became so miserable that I just wanted out of this cycle. I wanted to be "normal". My mother kept telling me, "Just get a grip, Laura." She would call from work when she knew I would be home and most likely eating. She tried to help me stop, but it only made it worse when she wasn't around because the compulsion to eat and get away with it was even stronger. Finally, Mom helped me to find a counselor. She made a point to find one that was a Christian. Initially we sat down together with her to give a history. This wasn't easy for either of us because we had to be vulnerable and air our dirty laundry. But I continued to go for individual sessions for a couple months and began to understand a little more about Eating Disorders. The counselor suggested the book <u>Fat is a Family Affair</u> to me by Judy Hollis (1985). I could finally see the dysfunction of my attitudes and actions. Hollis wrote, "When eating is accompanied by guilt, you're in trouble. Normal people don't eat with guilt. If they are going to be guilty, they simply refrain. E-D's project the guilt, wallow in it, beat themselves for it, and then eat anyway!" (p. 31-32). This certainly was me.

Hollis described a full-fledged compulsion, "Instead of going away, it gets worse. You continue eating until nauseated, even though food no longer works. You feel unable to cope emotionally, and to complicate things, you start having physical withdrawals periodically as you make futile attempts at testing your willpower. Even though food does not work, you have no other tools for coping, so you keep on the same merry-go-round, returning to food again and again" (p. 36). This was my story!

My counselor pointed me towards a 12 step program, Overeaters Anonymous (OA) during my senior year of high school. There were secret meetings held all over the city, usually in churches, or even libraries. Mom came with me to the first one to get me through the door. They would read excerpts from their literature, have someone share part of their story of their struggles with food. Then each person would introduce themselves in this way, "My name is Laura and I am a compulsive overeater (gulp). I have abstained from sugar and white flower for __ days." Sometimes they would share more about how they had struggled during the past week and if they overcame their temptations or not, with the help of their Higher Power. These meetings showed me that I was not alone. At first, they looked at me funny because I didn't look like I had a weight problem, and I was so young. But we had some of the same stories. We all had the same dysfunctional relationship with food and needed help breaking our habits. I was encouraged by the victories that they shared and gained strength from our common goals. This program gave me a handle on some of my compulsions and I began improving.

I thought about leaving all that behind when I went off to college for a fresh start, hoping I wouldn't need it anymore; as if I was moving away from my problems. However, my mother insisted that I continue finding OA meetings into college. Of course she was afraid that I would fall back into my old patterns without her nearby for support. At her insistence I searched out meetings in Cincinnati and I began attending them up to 3x a week. I eventually asked a woman named Kim to be my sponsor. I was asked to call her everyday as I worked through the steps. I read to her my daily food plan for accountability, and read my journal entries for the questions that guided me through the twelve steps. These questions helped me to think about and process some of the reasons why I was turning to food for comfort. What feelings were I trying to escape from when I looked for something that would satisfy me? According to the rules of the program, she was not supposed to give any feedback as I shared…no judgment. All she could do was listen. You maybe wondering what are these twelve steps, anyway?

The first 3 steps, to give you an idea, are found in the book The Twelve Steps and Twelve Traditions of Overeaters Anonymous (1995) published by Overeaters Anonymous Inc. They were the beginning of my way out of this pit."Step One. We admitted we were powerless over food—that our lives had become unmanageable." (p. 1)."Step Two. Came to believe that a Power greater than ourselves could restore us to sanity." (p. 9)."Step Three. Made a decision to turn our will and our lives over to the care of God as we understood Him." (p. 19).

In high school, I had to tell Brian about my secret as my evenings were taken with counseling sessions or meetings. He didn't pretend to understand what I was going through, and I probably told him as little as possible. It was such an embarrassing problem to have. But he did show me compassion, and supported my attempts to get to my meetings and call who I needed to call. He learned over time not to offer me food or make comments about what I was eating. But during our freshman year of college he could help. He had a car on campus and I did not. He was instrumental in driving me to my OA meetings. He would wait in the hallway for an hour or more and do his homework until I was finished. When I wanted to stop going because I thought maybe I didn't need it anymore, or because I was too embarrassed to face the roomful of people with my failures of the week, he insisted that I go.

Through this season in my life, God was using my struggles to draw me closer to Him. He allowed me to come face to face with my problems and weaknesses, and to see that my ways were not working. I was broken, and I had no idea how to fix myself. The journey I was on, including the programs and the people He placed in my life, showed me that I needed God. I like to say that it was my eating disorder that brought me to my knees. For the first time in my life I saw blatantly that I needed *Him*… not just the next binge, not a weight loss program, and not even a boy in love with me. I needed Jesus.

Three

Come to Jesus Moment

"Then Jesus declared, 'I am the bread of life.
Whoever comes to me will never go hungry, and
whoever believes in me will never be thirsty'" John
6:35

During our sophomore year of college, I had a *born again* experience with Jesus. I was in the depths of despair from this eating disorder. I had tried to do it on my own when I arrived at college. I think I believed that I had recovered enough to live a normal life. However, I quickly learned that this wasn't the case. My eating disorder felt like a monster within me. On one level I knew that I shouldn't turn to food; that it was no comfort at all. But there was a part of me that had an insatiable urge to indulge in food, maybe to escape feelings that I didn't want to deal with. I would tell my roommate Becky that I didn't need the snacks she kept on hand and offered me. But when I was alone I would sneak food out of her stash under her bed. I would return again and again to food, with virtually no willpower of my own to stop my addiction. I finally admitted that I needed help. As I returned to the OA meetings I began to have hope. I began to believe that Jesus was the only One who could heal and free me. I was right, by the way. I certainly couldn't heal myself. As much as Brian cared, he simply didn't understand my inner monster. My mother tried to help but was two hours away. Most of my friends didn't understand, or if they did, were dealing with the same temptations and had no solutions.

OA meetings pointed me to Jesus as my higher power, helping me realize that I had to start turning to Him in my moments of struggle. I started seeking Him. Sophomore year I joined a collegiate ministry called Navigators and met other believers like myself. I saw a hunger in these other students, and a fire in the leaders that I had never witnessed before. We worshipped together in the large group meetings, had small Bible studies, and I even found a mentor to disciple me.

Theresa was the leader of my Bible study which met in my dorm. She had such a love for Jesus and really seemed to care about all the girls in the study. She was so thorough as she led us through Bible passages and asked real questions. She took the time to get to know each one of us, and she offered to meet one on one with me to disciple me. This was a concept the Navigators' ministry strongly promoted as a way to teach new believers how to live a Christian life. Theresa was a few years older than I was and was married. She was open and honest about her life and her weaknesses. She could relate to my struggles with food and with body image. She could counsel me in my relationship with Brian and seemed to understand our temptations. She taught me how to pray out loud, how to study the Bible and how to lead a small group. We would meet at her house, at a coffee shop, or at the Christian bookstore. She helped me find a Study Bible with footnotes to explain the verses.

I began reading the Bible regularly, pouring over the verses and highlighting what stood out to me. I finally began to understand passages I'd heard all my life. The light came on. I finally "got" the gospel message and asked Jesus to be Lord and Savior of my life.

My binges grew further apart but I still messed up. I remember being really frustrated one night as I turned to God for forgiveness again for the same sin. I flipped open my Bible, aimlessly, trying to land on a verse that might be an encouragement, hoping that God would guide me somehow. I don't remember what the first several verses I landed on said as I flipped through the Old and New Testaments, but they all had to do with people sinning, angering God and getting punished somehow. I was so distraught. How were these stories supposed to help me now? I knew I messed up and deserved God's wrath and His punishment. I kept doing the same thing over and over even when I knew it was destructive and wrong. And then I saw it. I flipped one more time and found the beautiful Romans 5:8. *"But God demonstrates His own love for us in this. While we were still sinners, Christ died for us."* Yes. Yes! That was it! He died for me *while* I was still messing up. That's why I needed Him. His grace began to wash over me and the shame slipped away. Over time, the sin lost its grip on me as I continued to turn to and trust in Jesus.

I expected my soul mate to jump on the bandwagon with me as I spoon fed him every exciting detail of my new walk with the Lord. He didn't. Not yet, anyways. God was opening my eyes to so many things. He was gently convicting me, not only in the area of my food addiction, but also in my boundaries with Brian in our relationship. I began to see our physical feasts as the sin that they were and I started to pull back. As I told him, "Brian, we can't do sexual things anymore," he actually laughed because he said he knew it was coming. He agreed to this challenge and lovingly supported my changes, but watched from the sidelines.

"Therefore, if anyone is in Christ, he is a new creation; the old has gone, the new has come."
2 Corinthians 5:17

Now the challenge truly began for us as we slowly converted from having a worldly relationship to a Christian relationship, learning how to place God in the center and what to do with ourselves. It wasn't easy and I didn't find a lot of guidance on exactly how to practically do this. Later in our marriage, as I reflected on that season in college, I felt that God impressed upon me the desire of writing this book. I am confident that many of you have found yourselves at a similar crossroads in your dating relationship and my heart goes out to you. I want you to learn from our mistakes and our successes. I hope my children can learn from our story as well.

While Brian was still reading the fine print on Christianity, unable to see his need for Jesus, he did admit to me that he could see the benefits of sexual purity in our relationship. Now when we were alone we went *out* on dates! We found mutual hobbies and we talked—oh did we talk! I probably did 75% of it. We were growing now emotionally and most importantly, spiritually together. We talked about our future together, how many kids we wanted, what our pasts had been like.

Our physical relationship was taken out of the spotlight, but it was no easy task. While Brian was supportive, he wasn't sold out on the idea of purity for himself, from his own convictions. And while it was nice to not have to worry so much about how I looked for him, I was not getting physical reinforcement of his feelings for me through affection. The hardest part of our new lifestyle was that we knew exactly what we were missing, yet the temptations were still there. We had to decide where to draw the line physically. Sometimes we failed.

Brian did become a Christian after about a year, and over the years, God has made him into the spiritual head of our marriage and family. He has God's wisdom, a servant's heart, and a yearning for the Word. But that certainly didn't happen overnight. During our Sophmore year at Xavier, Theresa, my mentor, had introduced us to a Vineyard Church in Cincinnati. This was a new experience for both of us because it was a casual church that was very relatable. The format was simple, relevant and had inspiring messages. Now we could both begin learning side by side. Over the course of the next summer vacation, we started to visit churches in Indianapolis, to try to find one that he was interested in. I told him that as long as it was Christian I would go to any one of his choosing. Many of those churches ended with an altar call. Each time a preacher said that invitation I would glance at Brian, maybe even squeeze his hand to prompt him, but he never made a move. Finally, he agreed to go to a Billy Graham Crusade with me. I warned him that there would be an altar call... oh would there be one! I vowed to not pressure him this time and I even forced myself to keep looking forward as Graham pulled on everyone's heart strings at the end. As people from all over the arena began trailing down, I heard Brian quietly say, "I want to go down there."

Trying to hold back my shock and skepticism, I replied, "For me, or for you?"

He answered, "For me."

"Do you want me to come with you?" I asked.

"Yes!" he said emphatically.

He prayed *the sinner's prayer* on the floor of the arena, led by a volunteer, while holding my hand. He admitted his need for God, his belief in Jesus as his savior, and asked for forgiveness. These were words I had been longing to hear him pray for so long; I could have fainted. As we left that place, wading through the crowd, after I mentally picked myself up off the floor, the Holy Spirit spoke very clearly to my heart, "You can step down now."

What did this mean? You see, up to that point, I had been the spiritual leader of our relationship. God was reassuring me that He would mold Brian into the spiritual leader I desired to have. But He couldn't raise him up until I stepped down. A yoke was removed from my shoulders and God was asking me to trust Him to draw Brian near.

I saw glimpses of this beginning even that night. Brian had the idea after the Crusade to stop at a Christian coffee shop where we heard a live band play "He Ran to Me" and several other worship songs. Back at school, he joined a Navigators' Bible Study with other guys. Once in a while I would catch Brian saying something that struck me as really wise and out of character for him. I could begin to see the hand of God in his heart.

But several months later I was a little discouraged by his lack of growth. He didn't seem as interested in the Bible study, or Navigator functions... even church. During that time, in the Fall of our Junior year of college, I read an amazing book called <u>Lady in Waiting</u> by Debby Jones and Jackie Kendall.

It encouraged me to view myself as single again instead of attached already to Brian. This book changed my life and our relationship. I started re-evaluating if Brian was really meant for me. I kept praying, "God I want him to be the one, but if it's not your will please take him from me." I began to trust God with my future. I prayed this way every day for months. All I could ever hear in response, if anything, was "Wait, and just watch what I do." I eventually learned that I was actually getting in the way of Brian experiencing God for himself. I began to back off and tried to stop pressuring him. I stopped asking what he thought of the message at church, or if he was reading his Bible.

Here was a turning point. We were on a date at a restaurant, and over pizza he started discussing how all his friends went as far as to sleep with *their* girlfriends and how frustrated he was because, "I feel guilty for wanting to grab my girlfriend's butt." Well, I believe the Spirit of God was with me because I firmly told him that we were *not* married and this was not *his* body but mine, and he had *no* rights to touch me. I reminded him of the positive benefits we'd had from abstaining and why God asks us to be pure and keep the marriage bed sacred, and if he wanted it *that* bad he could find someone else who would give it to him. I fully expected him to walk away and I was strong enough in that moment to let him go. But he didn't, saying instead, "I just needed to be reminded."

"Forget the former things, do not dwell on the past. See, I am doing a new thing! Now it springs up; do you not perceive it?"
Isaiah 43:18-19

We got engaged a few months after that and had a 17-month engagement. On our wedding day we had gone two years without seeing each other unclothed. God had restored our purity and we were joined at that altar without shame. Now, we have been married for over 17 wonderful years. We have experienced true unity in God's sacrament of marriage. We feel God's blessing in our lives and in our relationship and we are even more excited about our future together with God. We have three amazing children. Brian and I both feel that the ways that God helped us to seek purity during our dating relationship have given us a strong foundation for a secure and committed marriage together. And you wouldn't believe how good the forbidden fruit tastes when God picks it from the tree, hands it to you, and says, "Here. This is my gift to you. It's no longer forbidden. You can partake of this gift without shame now."

Four

Play By the Rules

What Should a Christian Dating Relationship Look Like?

"How can a young person stay on the path of purity? By living according to your word. I seek you with all my heart; do not let me stray from your commands. I have hidden your word in my heart that I might not sin against you" Psalm 119:9-11

A Christian dating relationship is no different than any other aspect of Christian life in that it should reflect Jesus' Biblical teachings. In other words, we should play by His rules; not the rules of the 21st century society. It is in knowing God's Word in our hearts and choosing to live by His standards that we are able to lead pure lives.

In order to be 100% dedicated to the idea of purity it's important to look to the Bible to understand why it is so necessary. I came to realize that a strong foundation needed to come from reading and understanding God's instructions. Let's see what Jesus had to say about living out your relationships by His standards laid out in God's Word.

In Matthew 8:24-27 Jesus said, *"Therefore, everyone who hears these words of mine and puts them into practice is like a wise man who built his house on the rock. The rain came down, the streams rose, and the winds blew and beat against that house; yet it did not fall, because it had its foundation on the rock. But everyone who hears these words of mine and does not put them into practice is like a foolish man who built his house on sand. The rain came down, the streams rose, and the winds blew and beat against that house, and it fell with a great crash."*

Jesus' teachings, other Scriptures about purity, as well as Christian living in general, make up a foundation on the rock. Looking to our culture instead, or making decisions based on the feelings and desires of the flesh, is building a foundation in the sand. It simply won't last. Though we may be aware that these influences make for shaky ground, images bombard us through television, radio, merchandise, and books. The voice of the culture shouts at us through friends and possibly family members, and often encourages us to enjoy being young, and to give in to our sensual temptations. It's a current that is quite honestly very hard to say "no" to, and the pressures around us can wear us down over time.

In his book, Love, Sex and Relationships, Dean Sherman (1999) writes about the damage done when we don't follow God's rules about keeping sex within a committed marriage relationship (p. 79-92). He discusses how sex is meant to be rooted in deep love and commitment. When you begin a relationship with sex, it is actually based on excitement and newness. Eventually this excitement wears off, leaving a feeling of emptiness in the absence of true love and commitment. This reminds me of the sand Jesus spoke of, being washed away with the tide.

Several years ago, I had a friend who was fairly new in her Christian faith that was beginning a dating relationship. She was torn herself on where to draw the physical line and how far to go with this new love interest. I took a risk and spoke very candidly to her. I said, "You have a choice to make. Are you, or are you not going to trust and obey God? You can't say to God, 'I don't want to do it your way—I want to do it my way,' blatantly choose to disobey Him, and then expect Him to bless your relationship. You will either walk the path of obedience and blessing, or disobedience and heartache."

You wouldn't be reading this book if you were not at a crossroads. I come alongside you as an ally and sister in Christ and say this: The rewards that come from a house that stands through the storms far outweigh the pleasures of instant gratification. Remember that the house Jesus spoke of which was built on the sand fell with a great crash. Here are four rules I see based on the teachings in Scripture:

1. Don't play house
2. Monitor your modesty
3. Don't cross the line
4. Don't go it alone

Let's look at each of these in detail.

Rule One: Don't Play House

It is so common in our society for a dating couple to move in together, or cohabitate. According to an article by Amy Trace (2008) from *Focus on the Family* about half of all couples live together now before they marry. They may share some possessions, financial responsibilities, chores, and all leisure activities. Why don't they just tie the knot first? They want to see if the shoe fits. It's a temporary mentality which is very dangerous thinking, and not only from a spiritual perspective. It's a semi-commitment with an escape hatch. What was once a firm line of distinction between the laid back atmosphere of dating and the forever commitment and responsibilities of marriage, is now a hazy gray zone which may go on for years. The rationalization is that a couple can be more certain of their choice in their spouse if they move in together first. However, many enter their marriages with the same dating mentality of, "Well, if it doesn't work out..." So, due to the fear that we may end up with the wrong person and be unhappy and trapped, we rob ourselves of a deep love and commitment by leaving the back door ajar.

I was definitely guilty of *playing house* even though we weren't living together. I made the mistake of rationalizing sinful behavior in our relationship by applying Biblical verses about *marriage* to our *dating* relationship. I felt that since he would be my husband soon enough I should treat him as such and show the full extent of my love to him. Why was this a bad idea? First, there was no guarantee that Brian and I would actually get married, so we were committing fornication by engaging in sexual sin with a partner who was potentially someone else's spouse. Secondly, we were cheapening the sanctity of God's plan for the marriage relationship. I believe that if I had possessed a better understanding of God's perfect design for marriage, I would have drawn a firmer line in my mind between premarital and marital relationships. The threat to our healthy, lasting marriages is not uncertainty regarding the right spouse; rather it lies with a failure to implement the right plan. So let's get a better appreciation for God's design for relationships in the beginning.

Scripture tells us in Genesis 1:27-28, after God created the earth, "*So God created mankind in his own image, in the image of God he created them; male and female he created them. God blessed them and said to them, 'Be fruitful and increase in number; fill the earth and subdue it...'*"

Later in Genesis 2:18-25 is a recording of God's intention. "*The Lord God said, 'It is not good for the man to be alone. I will make a helper suitable for him...*" Then, after Adam named all the animals and found no suitable helper there, "*...the Lord God caused the man to fall into a deep sleep; and while he was sleeping, he took one of the man's ribs and closed up the place with flesh. Then the Lord God made a woman from the rib he had taken out of the man, and he brought her to the man. The man said, 'This is now bone of my bones and flesh of my flesh; she shall be called 'woman,' for she was taken out of man.' For this reason a man will leave his father and mother and be united to his wife, and they will become one flesh. The man and his wife were both naked, and they felt no shame.*"

I see a number of things in these passages. Firstly, God created man and woman in His own image. God is a relational being with the Father, the Son, and the Holy Spirit and He created mankind to be relational. He said, "It is not good for the man to be alone." Therefore, He made a helper suitable for him; a companion in Eve to walk alongside him. She complements his weaknesses with her strengths, and vice versa. Together they have a mission, given by the Lord, in caring for His creation. Marriage is meant to be a blessing to each partner, for companionship and for help in accomplishing God's purposes in our lives.

Secondly, He sets up the statute for marriage that a husband leaves father and mother to cling to his wife and be united with her. In other words, a husband and wife's loyalty is to each other, above and beyond their loyalty to their parents. It doesn't mean that their parents are no longer important or appreciated. Rather, this is an opportunity to take two people with different histories and cultures and fashion a new culture together. The lighting of the unity candle at wedding ceremonies is symbolic of this concept.

Lastly, God seems to want us to know that they were naked and felt no shame. Within a marriage, there is no shame in our nakedness. Our bodies belong to one another and it is the Lord's design that we be united as one flesh. I believe this unity in marriage refers not only to the physical act of sex, but beyond. A husband and wife become *one* spiritually as they walk together with God. We become *one* emotionally as we share one another's pains, joys and dreams. We become *one* family as we embark on life together, creating our own traditions, customs, and memories.

We see this beautiful design and intention continue into the New Testament. In Matthew 19 when the religious leaders asked Jesus about divorce, He quoted the Genesis passage above and said "*So they are no longer two but one flesh. Therefore what God has joined together, let no one separate*" (Matthew 19:6). Jesus affirms what God the Father set forth from the beginning in the unity of marriage.

The writer of Hebrews tells us, "*Marriage should be honored by all, and the marriage bed kept pure, for God will judge the adulterer and the sexually immoral"* (Hebrews 13:4). This speaks clearly against sex outside of marriage. It affirms sexual relations within the marriage relationship and calls for protection for this institution.

In the Book of Ephesians, Paul uses the following passage as an analogy for Christ and His church: *"Wives, submit to your husbands as to the Lord. For the husband is the head of the wife as Christ is the head of the church, his body, of which he is the Savior. Now as the church submits to Christ, so also wives should submit to their husbands in everything. Husbands, love your wives, just as Christ loved the church and gave himself up for her to make her holy, cleansing her by the washing with water through the word, and to present her to himself as a radiant church, without stain or wrinkle or any other blemish, but holy and blameless. In this same way, husbands ought to love their wives as their own bodies. He who loves his wife loves himself. After all, no one ever hated his own body, but he feeds and cares for it, just as Christ does the church—for we are members of his body. 'For this reason a man will leave his father and mother and be united to his wife, and the two will become one flesh.' This is a profound mystery—but I am talking about Christ and the church. However, each one of you also must love his wife as he loves himself, and the wife must respect her husband"* (Ephesians 5:22-33).

These are some difficult words to understand but they hold strong messages for us. The marriage relationship is a reflection of the unity between Jesus and His church, for whom He laid down His life. The Church doesn't question the authority and leadership of Christ but the Bride knows that He has her best interest at heart. This is a high calling and image for us to uphold in our marriage relationships. Imagine the beauty of a marriage in which the husband cares for and protects his wife as he would his own body, to the point of being willing to die for her. Imagine a wife having so much love and respect for her husband that she can bring every matter of her heart before him and trust in his loving guidance and leadership in her life. I believe this formula works best only when both partners are submitting to Jesus as Lord of their lives. I also believe that this unity in a Christian marriage is fused by the supernatural power of the Holy Spirit. This same spiritual unity is not present in a premarital relationship. Also, this kind of love is difficult to produce amidst a trial "we'll see if it works out" commitment.

In conclusion, rule number one is: Don't play house. Stand on the Rock of the Word of God in keeping the marriage bed pure. Protect the sanctity of marriage by not playing "husband and wife" until God seals your unity as you say your vows on your wedding day. Finally gain a full understanding of God's design in the unity of a husband and wife, within a marriage, to be a beautiful reflection of Christ and His Bride, the Church.

Rule Two: Monitor Your Modesty

Draw attention to the Holy Spirit at work in you; not to your body which houses it. Dress modestly. You can flatter your figure without drawing attention to it. Paul in the New Testament writes, *"I also want women to dress modestly, with decency and propriety, not with braided hair or gold or pearl or expensive clothes, but with good deeds, appropriate for women who profess to worship God"* (1 Tim 2:9).

Peter writes, *"Your beauty should not come from outward adornment, such as braided hair and the wearing of gold jewelry and fine clothes. Instead, it should be that of your inner self, the unfading beauty of a gentle and quiet spirit, which is of great worth in God's sight. For this is the way the holy women of the past who put their hope in God used to make themselves beautiful..."* (1 Peter 3:3).

This doesn't mean that you can't wear expensive clothes or jewelry or that they're inherently bad. In fact, God compares the nation of Israel to a woman and describes how He adorns her with beautiful clothes and jewelry as an analogy for His care and blessings upon her (Ezekiel 16: 9-14). What Paul and Peter are stressing is that we not draw more attention to our outward appearance than to our inward character. While we may be physically attractive, our true beauty should come from what the Holy Spirit is doing in our hearts.

Now I must admit here that I certainly was guilty of placing too much emphasis on my physical appearance. I think that is one thing that contributed to my eating disorder I described earlier. Even now, in my late 30's I cringe when I leave the house without makeup on. In her book, <u>Lies Women Believe</u>, Nancy Leigh DeMoss says, "The deception that physical beauty is to be esteemed above beauty of heart, spirit, and life leaves both men and women feeling unattractive, ashamed, embarrassed and hopelessly flawed. Ironically, the pursuit of physical beauty is invariably an unattainable, elusive goal—always just out of reach" (p. 78).

Of course every girl wants to feel pretty. The issue is where does your value lie? When someone meets me for the first time, I'd much rather they think to themselves, "Wow, what a godly woman!" instead of, "Wow, what a pretty face!" Likewise, your dating partner should be drawn to your inward character above and beyond your outward appearance. It's something that will not only last forever but will improve with age under God's control, unlike the latter.

If it sounds like I'm picking on women here, well, I am. I used to struggle with this myself. We, women, are taught by society to wield our appearance like a trap. It's not that our intentions are always bad, it's just that we long to be noticed and to feel desirable. Unfortunately, we often derive our self-worth from the attention we can draw to our outward appearance, instead of the unfading beauty of a gentle and quiet spirit of which Peter speaks. What some of us women don't realize, and my husband has confirmed for me, is that men are very visually stimulated. We think we're just getting his attention by using our physical attributes, but in fact we are creating a snare for our fellow Christian brothers. Jesus shed some light on the subject in Matthew 5:28: *"But I tell you that anyone who looks at a woman lustfully has already committed adultery with her in his heart."* As I grew closer in my walk with the Lord I began to have a desire to protect Brian's purity as well as my own, and not tempt him more than he could handle. I didn't want to stand in the way of Brian getting closer to God himself.

I want to point out the story of Bathsheba and King David in 2 Sam 11. We often hear this story in a sermon on lust because David sees this woman bathing on her rooftop and ends up sleeping with her, impregnating her, and then orchestrating her husband's death in battle. If you aren't familiar with the story, please read it in its entirety in 2 Samuel 11-12. It's really eye opening, but have your box of tissues nearby. In the end, there are some tough consequences as a result of God's justice on David. But what about Bathsheba's role in these events? According to the Holman Bible Dictionary (p. 156), complete bathing was rarely done in the Middle Eastern culture. Most references in the Bible to someone taking a bath were around a water source, and more often only partial bathing was done for ceremonial purposes. Did Bathsheba have to be bathing on the rooftop for all to see? Or could she have done her ritualistic washing inside? David was definitely in sin, but she may have had a part in it too. Had she practiced modesty, she would've most likely avoided alluring King David, an unexpected pregnancy, and the death of her husband that followed.

Thus, rule number two: Don't show off. Monitor your modesty. lest there be bloodshed. Think about what you can do to help protect your brother in Christ, whether it be change how you dress, or how you carry yourself.

Rule Three: Don't Cross the Line

The apostle, Paul writes to the Church in Galatians 5:16-26 about living by the Spirit and what that looks like. *"So I say, live by the Spirit, and you will not gratify the desires of the sinful nature. For the sinful nature desires what is contrary to the Spirit...The acts of the sinful nature are obvious: sexual immorality, impurity, and debauchery; idolatry and witchcraft, hatred, discord, jealousy, fits of rage, selfish ambition, dissensions, factions, and envy; drunkenness, orgies, and the like...But the fruit of the Spirit is love, joy, peace, patience, kindness, goodness, faithfulness, gentleness and self-control..."*

Those are convincing words but not very specific instructions when we are trying to figure out how far we can go without sinning. The Bible doesn't tell us exactly how and where we are allowed to touch one another. Let me remind you once more of the words of Jesus in Matthew 5:27-28. He told His listeners, *"You have heard that it was said, 'Do not commit adultery.' But I tell you that anyone who looks at a woman lustfully has already committed adultery with her in his heart."*

What exactly is lust? According to the dictionary, lust is a strong feeling of sexual desire (Merriam-Webster's Dictionary). God is concerned with our heart's condition. If we allow ourselves to be overcome with lust for one another, not only are we opening a door for the temptation of acting out against the best interests of our loved ones, but we've already sinned in God's sight. When our focus is on self-gratification and seeking pleasure, we are tying the hands of the Holy Spirit in our relationships. How can you embody the fruits of the Spirit and serve your future mate as Christ loves the Church if you're allowing yourself to be overcome with sexual desires?

Don't fool yourself into thinking the issue here is that you're just so in love and destined for marriage that you can't keep your hands off of each other. I'm sure I told myself that in our dating years. The issue is, rather, with self-control and self-discipline. If you cannot relinquish control of your flesh to the Holy Spirit in your lives now, this spiritual battle will not automatically be conquered the night you say "I do." You will likely continue to deal with temptations of the flesh even into your marriage. Conquer it now with God's help or you'll be dealing with temptations down the road that are beyond the safe limits of marriage.

I read about this very idea in one of my favorite dating books: "A woman subconsciously wonders, 'If he did not exhibit self-control with me before marriage, how can I be sure that he will not give into temptation during marriage when an attractive younger woman comes along?' A young man who cannot control himself before marriage does not suddenly become a man of self-control because he wears a wedding band!" (Kendall, 1995, p. 94).

Seek God's guidance on where to draw the line of purity in your dating relationship. I can't tell you exactly where it should be. This may depend on your levels of temptation. You may not be able to be completely alone at first without giving in. I can say that you should avoid anything that causes arousal for either party. Stay fully clothed and don't touch anything "where the sun don't shine." That's just plain common sense, though more than I had at one time.

In any case you need to draw the line in the sand and vow not to cross it. In fact, I've given you the opportunity to write it down on paper at the end of this chapter. It's that important! A recurrent theme in the Book Song of Songs is, *"Daughters of Jerusalem, I charge you, by the gazelles and by the does of the field; Do not arouse or awaken love until it so desires"* (Song of Songs 3:5).

Have a conversation together about where you think that line in the sand needs to be drawn, and respect each other's limitations. One may feel a need to stop at kissing, while another at full body hugs. Pray about this decision separately and with each other. You may need to make adjustments as you go. Don't focus on what you think you're missing, but rather on the fact that you're protecting the sanctity of your future marriage. Think of what you're preserving. You can spend the rest of your married life together exploring God's sexual gifts to one another. After giving it some prayerful thought, sign your purity commitments at the end of this chapter and vow to follow Rule three: Don't cross the line in the sand.

Rule Four: Don't Go It Alone

Accountability is so important for helping a dating couple honor a commitment to purity. I recommend each one of you have an accountability partner that you call regularly or after each date. Ecclesiastes 4:10 says, *"If one falls down, his friend can help him up. But pity the man who falls and has no one to help him up!"* You're less likely to cross that boundary when you know you have to fess up to someone else. Obviously you should choose carefully who you trust as an accountability partner. I'm not suggesting you should put an ad in the paper, but search for someone that has the following criteria: That person should be of the same sex as you, holding to the same Christian values you're striving for, rooted in Scripture, and one who has practiced and experienced purity. That doesn't mean your accountability partner is perfect. In fact, if he or she can be transparent with you, then you will learn from his or her mistakes.

You might ask, "Why can't my boyfriend and I just be accountable to each other?" You and your dating partner can be accountable to each other for a number of things, but not so with this subject of physical temptation. Your carnal natures will run off with each other. It didn't help me to hear directly from my fiancé that he was feeling tempted, drawn by my beauty, and barely able to contain himself. While it was nice to hear, it made me weak in the knees and vulnerable to rationalizing sin.

Become aware of when you're most vulnerable to temptation. Pay attention to your emotional state. For example, if you're feeling lonely, stressed out, unattractive, etc., you can tell your honey about it. Then he or she can *verbally* build you up and you can pray together. You see, once you take out that physical component you may have turned to in the past, you are forced to use other, healthier means to build one another up. Fine tuning these skills of verbal communication will only benefit you later on as your relationship progresses.

Along with this topic of accountability I feel I should mention the need to monitor the kinds of movies you watch and types of media you expose yourselves to. Obviously, seeing nudity on the screen won't help you take your mind off physical encounters. I had to guard myself from looking at the covers of secular magazines in the grocery stores that displayed seductive pictures. They are hard to avoid in the checkout line. Seeing them caused me to compare myself to those airbrushed models. This made me doubt myself which, in turn, tempted me to seek affirming attention from Brian.

If either of you has a possible sexual addiction, with pornography or other means, this is the time to seek help through accountable Christians, support groups, Christian literature, and Christian counseling if possible. There is more help available than ever before. Honesty, grace, and forgiveness are musts on all sides. The power to give your partner that honesty, grace, and forgiveness, whether you're doing the confessing or receiving it, must come from Jesus. Sexual addiction, either at present or from your past, will cripple your relationships and your life. It will rob you and your future spouse of a joyful marriage. While not impossible to overcome, you can't expect to break free on your own.

If you don't have someone in your life that can relate, Sexaholics Anonymous may be a place to start. It is "A fellowship of men and women who share their experience, strength and hope with each other so they may overcome their sexual addiction and help others recover from sexual addiction or dependency" (International Service Organization of SAA, 2007-2016). They use a version of the 12 steps from Alcoholics Anonymous to promote recovery through confidential small groups.

So why do we have to expose these vulnerable parts of our private lives with another uninvolved person? Iron sharpens iron. We see this in multiple examples throughout the Bible with Naomi and Ruth, Jonathan and David, and Saul even had Samuel. The Body of Christ should work as a body with each part supporting each other. James 5:16 says: *"Therefore confess your sins to each other and pray for each other so that you may be healed. The prayer of a righteous person is powerful and effective."*

We also see a principle of discipleship in 2 Timothy 2:2: *"And the things you have heard me say in the presence of many witnesses entrust to reliable people who will also be qualified to teach others."* I learned about this concept of discipleship or mentoring through the collegiate ministry I was involved in called the Navigators. Mentoring goes a step further than accountability. An accountability partner is someone who's walking alongside you on your road to know Jesus better. You're essentially equally yoked as friends. A mentor is a person who is a step or two ahead of you, someone who has a little more wisdom and experience to impart to you. You set aside time to meet with your mentor and share your lives, experiences and insights with each other as you study Scripture and grow in the spiritual disciplines together.

God placed a couple different mentors in my life at crucial times. They modeled for me how to pray, how to study Scripture, how to backup my convictions, and how to better my relationships. Usually these meetings happened over a cup of hot chocolate at a coffee shop, or in one of our homes. As a result, I felt like I wasn't alone and I had much needed guidance and direction in my life that was based in God's Word. Ultimately I began to have more success in having a Christ centered dating relationship.

Take the steps necessary in your life to follow Rule 4: Don't go it alone. Find yourself an accountability partner or even a mentor. I hope that I've given you some encouragement on your road to purity. Remember that the goal, as always, is to build your house on the rock.

His Purity Commitment

I, _____ vow to love and respect you,
(Your name)

_____, as the daughter of the
(Her name)

King and honor your purity. I vow to honor God's Word when He commanded that all sexual acts be reserved for the marriage relationship, so as to keep your marriage bed sacred and pure. I ask for your forgiveness for when I may have overstepped my bounds in sinful or lustful behavior, or used manipulation or guilt. With God's grace and help, I vow to treat you with the love of Jesus Christ, and to refrain from the following actions that may make you more vulnerable to temptation:

_____

_____

I voluntarily choose to remain accountable to _____
as well as to

God, Himself, to uphold this vital commitment to you.

_____   _____

(Your signature)   (Date)

Her Purity Commitment

I, _____ vow to love and respect you,
   (Your name)

_____, as the son of the King
   (His name)

and honor your purity. I vow to honor God's Word when He commanded that all sexual acts be reserved for the marriage relationship, so as to keep your marriage bed sacred and pure. I ask for your forgiveness for when I may have overstepped my bounds in sinful or lustful behavior, or used manipulation or guilt. With God's grace and help, I vow to treat you with the love of Jesus Christ, and to refrain from the following actions that may make you more vulnerable to temptation:

_____

_____

I voluntarily choose to remain accountable to _____ as well as to

God, Himself, to uphold this vital commitment to you.

_____   _____

(Your signature)   (Date)

Five

Placing God in the Center

"Do you not know? Have you not heard? The Lord is the everlasting God, the Creator of the ends of the earth. He will not grow tired or weary, and his understanding no one can fathom. He gives strength to the weary and increases the power of the weak. Even youths grow tired and weary, and young men stumble and fall; but those who hope in the Lord will renew their strength. They will soar on wings like eagles; they will run and not grow weary, they will walk and not be faint."
Isaiah 40:28-31

C hristianity should go beyond striving to follow the rules. Our real strength comes from hoping in the Lord, and placing Jesus in the center of every aspect of our lives.

In our dating relationships He becomes the central member. Jesus chastised the Pharisees time and time again throughout the New Testament for dedicating themselves to studying and enforcing the law and their man-made rules but not having a relationship with God. In Luke 11:42 He says, *"Woe to you Pharisees, because you give God a tenth of your mint, rue and all other kinds of garden herbs, but you neglect justice and the love of God…"* and in verse 52 He tells them, *"Woe to you experts in the law, because you have taken away the key to knowledge. You yourselves have not entered, and you have hindered those who were entering."*

The Law

The Law that God gives us is a good thing, right? It gives us guidelines, do's and don'ts, and shows us what God requires. But many of us, as human beings, want God to make everything black and white, don't we? We want some gauge or thermometer that tells us if we're good enough before God. Some of us, like the Pharisees, would reduce religion to just that: a thermometer that measures our spiritual temperature, even our worth. But that's not the intent of the Law. The heart of God's desire for us is not just that we get all the questions right and be A+ students in His class. He desires to change our hearts through a relationship with Him. Sure, He is pleased with our obedience—*when* it comes from a place of love and gratefulness as a response to His grace in our lives. However, obedience out of a mere sense of duty or, in some of the Pharisees' case, for the sake of appearances, is a hindrance to our true spiritual growth.

In Romans 3:20-24 the Apostle Paul explains, *"Therefore no one will be declared righteous in his sight by observing the law; rather, through the law we become conscious of sin. But now a righteousness from God, apart from the law, has been made known, to which the Law and the Prophets testify. This righteousness from God comes through faith in Jesus Christ to all who believe. There is no difference, for all have sinned and fall short of the glory of God, and are justified freely by his grace through the redemption that came by Christ Jesus."*

Jesus came to fulfill the Law. He is the key to knowledge that the Pharisees were missing. When you place your faith in Him and accept His gift of grace through His death and resurrection you are made righteous, period. Your righteousness is apart from the law, apart from your performance and effort. No matter how many times you fail, you are already righteous if you've put your faith in Him. He said in John 14:6, *"I am the way and the truth and the life. No one comes to the Father except through me."* Following the rules won't get us right with God. Having a relationship with Jesus will not only make us right with God, but will enable us to better keep the law and to recover after a fall. Jesus also said in John 15:5, *"I am the vine; you are the branches. If a man remains in me and I in him, he will bear much fruit; apart from me you can do nothing."*

So how do we place Jesus in our premarital relationships? Well, we must first place Him in the center of our lives as individuals; connect ourselves to the vine. Jesus must be your First Love. Your loyalty is ultimately to Him, not to your earthly partner. As I grow in my relationship with Him, I find myself longing to know His Word, His requirements. I want to obey Him, not to get that A+, but because I know that He loves me, I have grown to love Him and I want to honor my God.

Quiet Times

Cultivate your personal relationship with Jesus in the same way you would cultivate another relationship: through quality time. I can tell you from experience that you have far more time to do this as a single person than after you are married and having babies. As a wife and mother of three children, I have to be real creative at carving out time to meet with Jesus, but it refreshes and restores my soul to connect with my First Love.

I have always referred to my meetings with Him as my quiet times. There is not one right way to spend a quiet time but here are some ideas. If you are new to Christianity this may seem strange or foreign to you, but start by setting aside 10-15 minutes each day when you can focus on God without distractions. I recommend beginning the time by inviting the Holy Spirit to meet with you and reveal God's heart to you. Grab a Bible you can relate to and start with a book in the New Testament.

When you're beginning a relationship with Jesus read the first-hand accounts we have about Him in the Gospels. The Book of John was recommended to me early on as being easy to read and interesting. Read just one chapter or passage at a time and think about or meditate on a truth that stands out to you. What does it tell you about the character of Jesus or God the Father? What can you learn from Jesus' words or actions? How do they apply to your day? Being a Christian means becoming like Christ. What can you learn from the other characters in the story and how they are responding to God? I like to jot down my thoughts on paper. Next, let your time flow into prayer.

If you're not accustomed to praying out loud to God, you could start by journaling. I have journaled my prayers to God for years. I continue this practice because it helps me to focus my thoughts. I can read back over the months and years and

remember the wonderful things He's done in my life. I mark
the special ones that are especially dear to me.

Tell God what you're grateful for. Tell Him how you're
feeling. Be honest with God. If you're confused, feeling
distant, or angry tell Him openly. He knows already anyhow.
David poured His heart out to God in the Psalms of the Old
Testament. Give Him your desires. It's okay to ask God for what
you need or desire. If it is aligned with His will, He'll provide
it when the time is right.

Our prayers should also move beyond our own needs to
the needs of others and His Kingdom work. In this way we
aren't just focusing on what we want for ourselves from God,
but allowing our hearts to turn to what He would ask of us. For
example, how can I serve Him today by helping others, praying
for their needs, or being His light in the world I interact with?
How can I point those I encounter to His amazing love and
saving grace?

At the end of your prayer, reserve a couple minutes of silence
before God. Listen to His voice in your life. Borrow David's
prayer in Psalm 139:23-24: *"Search me, O God, and know my
heart; test me and know my anxious thoughts. See if there is any
offensive way in me, and lead me in the way everlasting."* You
may have some thoughts come to mind, or a single word or
picture given to you by the Holy Spirit; or you may simply feel
a peace come over you, calming your anxieties and the worries
you laid before Him. This is when I may feel God's gentle
conviction, asking me to make an apology for something I have
said in anger. He may soak an attribute of His character deep
into my heart.

Several years ago I was praying and staring out the window
of a hotel room. I noticed an American flag waving in the
breeze. As I sat in silence before God, He seemed to give me

these thoughts: "You can't see the wind, but by looking at that flag you know the wind is moving. It's invisible but you have no doubt that it's there. In the same way, no one can see the Holy Spirit. But when they look at your life they can tell that the Spirit is moving. Be like that flag, Laura. Be the evidence to those around you that my Holy Spirit is real." To this day when I see a flag waving in the breeze, I have a reminder to make sure I am living in such a way that others can know that God is real. This is aligned with scripture about living a fruitful life to point others to God (see Colossians 1:10, 1 Peter 2:12 and Galatians 5:16-26).

Developing a quiet time that suits you and your personality can take time and may seem awkward or tedious at first. But after some practice and some experiences with Jesus first hand, you will grow to crave and depend on this time with Him. Jesus said He knows His sheep and they know Him and will listen to His voice (see John 10:14-16). Before long, you will be going beyond the 15 minutes because of your own desire to be in His presence. You may even lose track of time.

The Big Picture

I recently unearthed one of my journals from 1999. This was the time in my life where I was really discovering what a relationship with Jesus could look like. Here is how I described my love relationship with the Lord at that time:

> "I call Him my First Love because I don't
> want anyone or anything else to come before
> Him; but I think maybe my actions aren't always
> in accordance. I am passionate about Him.
> When I hear His name my ears perk up. When

I hear His voice I am overcome with peace and
excitement. I love to read His love letter to me
(the Bible). However, I don't always give Him
the time and attention that I'd like to. I don't
always submit to Him or think of Him."

How do you develop a love relationship with the Lord?
It seems strange, but it's the same way you develop a love
relationship with a significant other. As I stated in the last
chapter, our marriage relationships on this earth are meant to
reflect the love between Jesus and the Church. Here are some
ideas I wrote in my 1999 journal on tangible steps I could take
to solidify a love life with the Lord:

- Spend more time completely focused on Him
- Pour out my feelings, worries, and cares
- Listen for His voice
- Read what He's written to me
- Write Him love letters
- Rejoice in what He's given me
- Talk about Him
- Become more like Him
- Submit to Him
- Serve Him
- Teach my children to respect Him
- Defend Him
- Be honest and real with Him
- Sing to Him
- Eat and drink with Him
- Trust Him

These are things I do throughout my day, beginning with a
quiet time. I talk to Him while driving in the car, or sing along

with the radio. I pray that He helps me to serve my patients in my Home Health job, and serve my children and husband as if I am serving Jesus Himself. I have gone to a coffee shop and sat down with my Bible, imagining Him across the table from me.

I talk about Him every chance I get. I love to wear cross necklaces because they are often conversation starters. I actually have an international cross collection from 8 different countries with a necklace from Mexico, South Korea, Japan, Germany, England, West Africa, Ireland and of course the United States. Each one has a story and can invite others to talk about their faith with me.

A new tradition I have begun is to take a full day when the kids are at school and spend it at a retreat center alone with God. I bring my Bible, notebook, and currently this book in progress. I spend extended time with Him praying, reading the Word and writing. Weather permitting, I may go on a walk with Him on one of their trails. I try to take one day during the season of Advent and one day during the season of Lent to get myself centered and my heart open for what He wants to teach me during the holiday. I may buy a small souvenir in the gift shop to remind me of a lesson learned. I always leave feeling so refreshed and uplifted and with my faith in God solidified.

Recently God gave me a special message through an unexpected avenue. I was unwrapping a Dove Dark Chocolate, looking forward to a little indulgence, and the wrapper said, "Sweep them off their feet." This really struck me as I immediately sensed God was trying to tell me something, and I wondered at the meaning. I knew that He was telling me to sweep my family off their feet, specifically my husband and children. It's a concept we think of when we are courting one another, but after so many years of doing life together, it fades into the background. He impressed a verse on my heart from 1

Peter 1:22-23 *"Now that you have purified yourselves by obeying the truth so that you have sincere love for your brothers, love one another deeply, from the heart. For you have been born again…"* I was convicted that I really am not good at sweeping them off their feet and loving them deeply from the heart. I am so focused on getting the job done, keeping things fair, not giving into every request so I don't spoil anybody, and keeping order in the house. Sweeping them off their feet feels so indulgent… like that piece of Dove chocolate. I asked the Lord to guide me in this. I was disheartened to realize how alien this concept was for me; how selfish I truly am. How do I begin to sweep them off their feet? What does this even look like? This is what I journaled as I prayed:

Sweep them off their feet

- Go above and beyond what's required or expected
- Put their needs before my own
- Enjoy them
- Serve them (identify their need and seek to meet it)
- Surprise them
- See the best in them as well as their potential
- Overlook offenses

This was such a gift to me from God in that Dove Chocolate wrapper. The chocolate I looked forward to was temporary. The spiritual lesson was sweet and eternal-life changing; a reminder that God still sees me and knows what I need. He gave me a mission for each day which is far more satisfying than the chocolate that I crave.

A Cord of Three Strands

*"Though one may be overpowered, two can defend themselves.
A cord of three strands is not quickly broken." Ecclesiastes 4:12*

Think of a cord of rope with three strands braided tightly together. This verse in Ecclesiastes is comparing a team or a friendship to that braided rope. When we stand alone, we are weak, but we know there is strength in numbers. Now imagine that this rope represents you and your partner with your lives intertwined together. The third strand is God, present in you both through the Holy Spirit. The Spirit of God should be woven into your relationship in this way, involved in every twist and turn. As you stand back and look at a rope, you no longer see three separate strands, but one unit.

Once you both are giving adequate attention to your individual relationships with Jesus, it will be much easier to place Him at the center of your shared time together. You can study God's Word together and pray together, out loud or in silence. Worship God together, whether that's going to a church service or singing along to a worship C.D. in the car. Talk about what God's doing in your hearts and in your lives. Most importantly, seek God's guidance for decisions you make together as a couple. Seek out and submit to His plans for your lives individually and together, and you will be filled with abundant joy as you watch God work.

God wants so badly to be intimately involved with you. If you trust Him with the details of your lives, over time, you will see He has your best interest at heart. Though, remember that His goal is not to pad your life with all the comforts and measures of success of our times. He is building your character, making you into the likeness of His Son, Jesus, and involving you in His great Kingdom work! So as you hand over the reins to Him, this is what you will see unfold in your lives.

The Apostle John, one of Jesus' 12 disciples, wrote three letters to some Gentile (non-Jewish) churches toward the end of his life. In the first letter, First John, he writes in detail of how God loves us and lives through us as we love others. In 1 John 4:9 he writes, *"This is how God showed his love among us: He sent his one and only Son into the world that we might live through him."* Later, in verse 13, he says, *"We know that we live in him and he in us, because he has given us of his Spirit."*

I wonder if, as he wrote this, he was picturing the conversation Jesus had with His disciples in the Gospel of John chapter 15, written by this same author. In this chapter Jesus used a beautiful piece of imagery, the vine and the branches, to describe the kind of relationship that we should have with Him. In verse 5 He says, *"I am the vine; you are the branches. If a man remains in me and I in him, he will bear much fruit; apart from me you can do nothing."*

The message we derive from the vine and branches analogy, and the cord of three strands, is that Jesus longs for us to abide in Him. We have access to Him, the author of all Creation, as a member of our team. Through the Holy Spirit working in and through us, we tap into His mighty power for our lives and our relationships. Why would the God of All stoop to our level in this way? Because He loves us with a perfect love. In John 15 verses 9-11 He continues, *"As the Father has loved me, so have I loved you. Now remain in my love. If you obey my commands, you will remain in my love, just as I have obeyed my Father's commands and remain in his love. I have told you this so that my joy may be in you and that your joy may be complete."*

He loves us with a love we cannot comprehend. He desires to have a close relationship with us, to see our joy complete in

Him, and to see us bear fruit that will last to bring glory to His Name. We respond to this outpouring of His love by allowing Him access to our lives and relationships. In this way, we honor Him by trusting in His goodness and His intentions for us. In doing so, we also experience freedom from the things which once held us in bondage.

In Beth Moore's book, <u>Breaking Free</u>, she explains how, in order to find true liberty and freedom in Christ, we have to submit every area of our lives to His authority, trusting His heart for us. Sometimes we find it easy to submit certain areas to Him, but not others. I know for myself, giving my relationship with Brian over to God was especially difficult. However, how could I experience the strength of three cords needed for that relationship unless I submitted to Jesus in this area?

Beth Moore writes in <u>Breaking Free</u>, "Until we choose to withhold no part of our lives from His authority, we will not experience full freedom." Then she goes on to describe that a life fully submitted to God's control is not without mistakes or suffering. "Obedience does not mean sinlessness but confession and repentance when we sin. Obedience is not arriving at a perpetual state of godliness but perpetually following hard after God. Obedience is not living miserably by a set of laws, but inviting the Spirit of God to flow freely through us. Obedience is learning to love and treasure God's Word and see it as our safety" (Moore, 2000, p. 179).

Maybe I found it difficult to surrender this area of my life to God because I knew I would still make mistakes. Also I was afraid of how Brian would react to me rejecting his physical advances. Would he completely lose interest and even break off the relationship in search of someone less prudish? Over time, I saw that God had grace and forgiveness for me as I kept pressing forward. Yes I did mess up at times, but I kept searching for His voice and trying to follow my Good Shepherd. I also saw that Brian had a heart for the Lord as well. He was taking steps to find out what God required of him and began learning, along with me, how to honor God in our relationship. He didn't leave me for someone else, and he didn't lose his attraction for me. He began to submit his own life to Jesus and sought to restore the purity that we had lost in our relationship. God did strengthen us and show us benefits of following His ways. We both learned how faithful and trustworthy our God was as we allowed our lives to be interwoven with His Spirit in a cord of three strands.

Six

What Do We Do With Ourselves?

"Flee from sexual immorality. All other sins a man commits are outside his body, but he who sins sexually sins against his own body. Do you not know that your body is a temple of the Holy Spirit, who is in you, whom you have received from God? You are not your own; you were bought at a price. Therefore honor God with your body." 1 Cor 6:18-20

If your dating experience has been anything like ours, you may be trying to make some changes in order to align your lives with God's will. I mentioned in "Our Story" that our relationship had diminished to a purely physical one as we traveled down the slippery slope of intimacy. It was hard to find sure footing to climb back to where we needed to be. Once we vowed to reclaim our purity, we found ourselves at a crossroads, asking, "What do we do with ourselves now?" Before we had a firm foundation in God's Word, we often failed in our attempts at purity because our flesh was too weak. We would fall back into old patterns. Also, we were unsure of proper boundaries and had little guidance from our peers. This is why having older mentors is a great idea.

My intention in writing this chapter was to give you some practical ways to invest in your dating relationship while protecting your purity. This is something I feel Brian and I needed desperately as we tried to forge a path against the natural fleshly desires we had awakened. We had to actually go *out* on dates and avoid the dark dorm room scene with pizza and a movie... and a couch. I challenge you to invest your time and energy into protecting your own purity and the purity of your partner. Be creative and let this list stir up your own ideas.

Budget Dates

Brian and I are all too familiar with these dates. It seems we've always been aware of how much our dates were costing us. The truth is some of our most romantic and meaningful moments have occurred when we were doing things that were absolutely free. What can I say? I'm a cheap date.

Incorporating budget dates into your relationship not only stretches your money, but also eases your transition into marriage. Let me explain. Once we got married, the structure of our time together flip flopped. Prior to the wedding, 80% of our time together was in the form of a date and 20% of our time was spent doing the mundane. Now that we share a home, have children, and numerous other responsibilities, roughly 80% of our time is mundane and only about 20% of the time is spent on a date. While I always loved the typical courtship date of dinner and a movie, I see the incredible value in learning to relate to each other while doing the cheap and mundane as well. Brian and I have learned to have fun even while grocery shopping with each other. We capitalize on the moments we have.

Here are some other ideas:

1. Go to a library together and check out a love poem book. Read poetry to each other from comfy library chairs. You'll have to whisper. Of course there's always the Song of Songs—a famous poem in the Bible, written by King Solomon about his relationship with a peasant girl. Just for fun try to find your favorite childhood book while you're there.

2. Watch the sunset together in a special place. You'll need a good view of the West and try to wait for a night with a few scattered clouds to add dimension. Enjoy this beautiful gift together from our awesome Creator and Artist as you talk about what God's doing in your lives. Believe me, talking about God always dispels inappropriate thoughts.

3. Have a "quiet time" together, or prayer time with God. Pick something from the Bible to study together and discuss. I know it doesn't sound romantic, but sometimes you just need an intellectually stimulating conversation. Not only that, but it can be so touching to hear what your loved one has to say to your Heavenly Father about you in prayer. So pray for each other, but watch where you lay those hands.

4. Walk a dog together or, better yet, a puppy. It doesn't even have to be yours; just ask first before you borrow your neighbor's pet. Watching someone interact with

an animal in a caregiving role gives a good indication of future parenting skills!

5. Play in the park. Push each other on swings and share the funny stories of your childhood mischief. I never get tired of hearing how Brian electrocuted himself at age thirteen. See how many different parks you can find over time near your town.

6. Go on a photo date where you snap pictures of each other all over the city and frame your favorites. Optional: you could bring a best friend to take the shots if you don't own a selfie stick or, like me, refuse to buy one. It might be safer than asking random strangers.

7. Speaking of pictures, reminisce over your photo albums or scrapbooks together; go as far back as those cute little baby shots. Compare goofy pre-adolescent pictures and find the weirdest hairdos. Get to know one another's family members. When you show up at his family gathering, they will be touched if you already know their names.

8. Find a spot near your airport where you can watch airplanes take off and land; get as close as you can. Talk about some of the places you've traveled to or where you hope to go one day.

9. Sell some books at a second hand store and buy something with your earnings. Get as close to the exact amount as you can.

10. Wash your cars together on a hot day. Soon a task that may have been boring can become fun while done together. Find out what he knows about cars. Does he change his own oil or leave it to a mechanic?

11. Ride bikes together. Wear helmets for safety and don't worry about the hair. Bring a snack along or stop along the way for a milkshake.
12. Play tennis together at a nearby school or park. You don't have to keep score or know all the rules.
13. Visit a farmer's market and look for local treasures. If it's later in the Fall look for an apple orchard, especially the one that lets you pick your own apples.
14. Attend a local theater production. We have found high schools to put on some impressive shows for just a few bucks. Those young actors and actresses certainly appreciate the crowd.

Group Dates

Group dates benefit a relationship in many ways. Sometimes it is great just to see how your loved one interacts with others. Also you might be a little nicer to one another in a crowd. A group setting where we were surrounded by friends always motivated me to watch my tongue and treat Brian with more respect. Also, it supported our purity. Let's be honest; there's safety in numbers.

Group dating is a good social investment. With dating, there's always the danger of getting so absorbed with each other that you lose some vital friendships as well as an outward focus. It's very valuable to have mutual friendships with other Christian couples. You can encourage one another in your trials, share similar visions, and pray for each other. Also, if you're focused on the needs of others you'll be less focused on your own physical temptations. Group dates give you the opportunity to invest in these friendships.

Here are some ideas for group dates:

1. Go hiking or canoeing with some friends. In fact, anything active is good for releasing all that pent up energy. Some fresh air just might do you some good! Be sure to pack a picnic lunch.

2. Get a game going with some friends, like basketball, tennis or soccer. You don't have to have skills to have a good time. Frisbees can be fun from simply tossing them, or with a larger group, play Frisbee golf or ultimate Frisbee. Ultimate Frisbee is kind of like soccer but you toss the Frisbee down the field to each other and past the goalie for points.

3. Make reservations for a group of friends at a family style restaurant. They serve too much for two anyways and fellowship is always a good thing. Be sure to sit next to your sweetheart. Decide ahead of time how you're going to split the bill.

4. Bring some younger cousins or siblings along to go horseback riding. Sometimes state parks have saddle barns. Or if you don't like horses, bring them to support a local church festival with rides. It's always a good idea for you and your partner to acquaint yourselves with each other's families.

5. Take a young child to a quiet fire station. If there are some trucks in the garage and firemen relaxing out front you can usually stop in for a free tour. Not only can you watch a small child's eyes light up, but you might learn some fun facts yourselves. And how will you know if your possible future husband is good around kids unless you see and observe him around kids?

6. Have a game night. Invite some friends over for appetizers and board games. Some of our favorites are Catch Phrase, Cranium, and Forbidden Island. Card

games are great as well. If you have a larger crowd you could organize a Euchre tournament. See how far you and your partner can go.

7. Find a spot to host a bonfire in early fall. Invite some Christian and non-Christian friends to the mix and see what conversations are sparked while roasting marshmallows. Better yet, add some guitar music or, if no one plays, a radio to help bring God into the atmosphere.

8. Movie night. Let's be honest, from here on out, your movies will have to be viewed in group settings. Whether you're at a movie theater, or cozy at home, there are just too many temptations when the lights go out. But oh so fun to bring a crowd of friends to a tasteful comedy or action flick. Ok, you can do a Rom-Com if you must, but keep your desires in check.

9. Meet up with some friends at a sporting event. This could be as simple as cheering on your Alma Mater's basketball team. Not only can it be fun and lighthearted, but you're supporting your old school. You could also seek out a professional team. Brian and I enjoyed a couple hockey games together. Not only were they entertaining, but fairly inexpensive.

Kingdom Dates

"But seek first His Kingdom and His righteousness and all these things will be given to you as well." Matthew 6:33

"These things" Jesus was referring to for his listening crowd, were their basic needs. He was assuring us that our Heavenly Father knows what we need even before we ask Him. We can trust His promise that, as we set our hearts and minds on His eternal purposes, He has our back. He will provide. Though you want to invest valuable time in your relationship together, God still has some awesome plans for you to take part in His Kingdom work at large.

This next list of date ideas will help you explore your own God-given design in the gifts He's given you individually, as well as His design for the two of you as a couple. This is the best way to find out if you have a heart for the same types of ministry. In the meantime, trust that He will take care of your relational needs.

1. Serve in your community together. Your church may have an outreach ministry you can get involved with, or you could do some acts of kindness on your own. Pass out free water bottles on a hot summer day with a note that says "Jesus loves you and will quench your thirst." Be sure to invite them to your church.

2. Visit people at a nursing home. You can just chat with those in the lobby. You could pass out some cheap trinkets or handmade cards. Play a board game with people hanging out in the Activities Room. Depending on your comfort level, you can ask the residents if there's anything you can pray about with them.

3. Volunteer at a soup kitchen or sort food and clothing for a charitable organization. These places often have a flood of volunteers around the holidays, but are in need of help throughout the rest of the year.

4. Participate in a blanket or coat drive, or organize one together.

5. Volunteer in your church's nursery or Children's Church. This can actually be a lot of fun. If your church

doesn't already have much in the way of Children's Church and you see a need for it, this is a great chance for you to be a creative pioneer.

6. Get to know the people on your streets. Pray about who you could reach out to. Bring brownies to a new family to welcome them to the neighborhood. Bring dinner to a family with a new baby; find an elderly couple that could use some help, the sky's the limit. Offer to rake leaves, shovel snow, go on a grocery run, or simply show up on the front door step with a meal. You might even get an opportunity to pray with someone.

7. Save up spare change and then drive around downtown to add change to people's parking meters. Leave a small card to let them know they've been loved on. A Vineyard church we used to attend uses the phrase "Showing God's Love in a Practical Way" when doing similar outreaches.

8. Offer to babysit for a young couple that you know and give them a date night. Many people don't have a good support network of family to help with this. Who knows, in a few years the tables may be turned.

9. Start a small group together and invite a mixture of people from your church and your neighborhood. Christian bookstores have scores of studies you can purchase, from books on relevant topics, to books of the Bible.

10. Evaluate together if there is an area of needed ministry that your church just isn't addressing. Pray about what God might put on your hearts and then do what you can to meet the need.

11. Pay for someone's meal or groceries that is standing behind you in a line.

12. Sit on a park bench in a public place with a $20 bill in your pocket, and pray together about who to give it to.
13. Bake some cookies together and bring them to the teachers at your old elementary school, or to a police or fire station. Thank them for their service.
14. To share an idea from a friend of mine, pass out simple cross necklaces to cashiers that help you with these words, "Here's a blessing from me and Jesus."

Alone-in-a-Crowd Dates

"How beautiful you are, my darling! Oh, how beautiful!..." Song of Songs 4:1

There's just something romantic about being alone in a crowd. How innocent when two people can gaze into each other's eyes and pour out feelings from their soul with no awareness of any bystanders. It's that idea of, "I don't care how goofy I look, I'm head over heels in love with you and I'm not ashamed to let the whole world see." I now understand why it was so important to Brian that I hold his hand in public.

Here are some ideas you can try for "Alone-in-a-Crowd" dates:

1. Have a candlelit picnic in a park. (A busy park. You know the rules—no going off in a remote state park to a secluded area.) You can get as fancy as chocolate covered strawberries and croissants or as relaxed as fried chicken. What a great opportunity to share prayer over the meal, be silly together, or talk about your future expectations.

2. Go out for coffee or hot chocolate in a fun coffee shop setting. You could read a devotional together or simply talk about your day. Speaking of devotionals, I highly recommend finding a Christian premarital workbook that can help you address all the little and big issues you'll face with possible matrimony. It's well worth the time, effort and small price to ensure you are both on the same page. Brian and I used Saving Your Marriage Before It Starts: Seven Questions to Ask Before—and After—You Marry by Dr. Les Parrott, and Dr. Leslie Parrott. (2015). Another suggestion is Fit to be Tied; Making Marriage Last A Lifetime by Bill and Lynne Hybels (1993).

3. Go out for ice cream. Pick a flavor that matches your personality and tell each other why as you slurp it up. Or pick a flavor that you think matches your honey's personality and explain why in a positive, affirming way. Is he simple and sweet like Vanilla, or athletic and protective like Superman?

4. Find some verses in the Bible that express the way you feel about each other and share them on a park bench. Ephesians 5:25 says: *"Husbands, love your wives, just as Christ loved the church and gave himself up for her…"* Therefore, any of the beautiful verses that describe God's love would be applicable. My husband and I chose a verse we liked and had the address inscribed on our wedding rings: *"Be imitators of God, therefore, as dearly loved children and live a life of love, just as Christ loved us and gave himself up for us as a fragrant offering and sacrifice to God"* (Ephesians 5:1-2). This was our reminder to try to imitate Jesus in our relationship with each other.

5. Eat take-out on one of your front porches where you can converse with neighbors and enjoy the weather. Neighborly relationships take work but are so valuable for a sense of community. God may have placed certain people right next door to you for a reason. Pray for ways to reach out to them.

6. Walk around a mall or shopping area together and compare tastes. You should know right here and now if there are styles you both enjoy. If not, who will get to do the decorating one day?

7. Go out for dinner at an authentic ethnic restaurant. Observe the customs and enjoy a new taste. It can be fun to try something different.

8. Go to a museum of your choice together to see and discuss how God has been active and involved in shaping history and creation since the beginning. Keep in mind, there are a lot of theories at those museums that are just that: theories. Well-meaning Christians have conflicting views on how to interpret the Bible's Creation account. If you and your dating partner disagree, explore your differences together. Don't let different viewpoints become divisive.

9. Go to a zoo together and observe and discuss how God has equipped each animal to survive its unique environment. What was with the ostrich, God?

10. Visit your County or State Fair. Be brave and ride some rides together. Pick an animal barn to "judge". Sometimes there are entertaining side shows.

Celebration Dates

"Place me like a seal over your heart, like a seal on your arm; for love is as strong as death..." Song of Solomon 8:8

These are dates for celebrating those special times— anniversaries, holidays, birthdays; you know, when you give yourselves permission to spend a little more money and go the extra mile. And why shouldn't you celebrate? God created us for relationships. Relationships that are full of selfless love for each other bring glory to their match-maker and creator. Praise God for the blessing of the special person in your life.

When we were dating and wanted to celebrate, we usually went somewhere special, and exchanged gifts and cards. I have a little advice regarding giving. First of all, I recommend Gary Chapman's book, <u>Five Love Languages.</u> (1995). It will help you discover your primary ways of giving and receiving love. If "giving gifts" is his love language, then make that a priority when you want to show him love. Make sure you're speaking each other's love language. Also, if your love language is "gifts" and his is "words of affirmation," give him a break when he doesn't naturally buy you a gift for your birthday but spends 20 minutes picking out just the perfect card to tell you how he feels.

Here are some ideas for celebratory dates:

1. Have dinner at a special place. We have a few favorite restaurants we like to frequent when we're celebrating. Sometimes it is fun to find a little family owned establishment to support with your patronage. If you become familiar with the servers or owners, you might find opportunities for spiritual conversations in time. It's a fun way to support a hard-working family business and

get close enough to make a spiritual impact together. If you make a habit of praying together before meals in public, you'll never know the changes you might inspire in quiet onlookers.

2. Spend the day downtown. Indianapolis has a canal walk where you can rent paddle boats during the day. Maybe your city has something similar. Find a yummy food truck. End the evening with a romantic carriage ride.

3. Don't forget about the theater. Anyone can take her to a movie, guys. Why not wow her with a symphony or theatrical performance? We both enjoyed A *Christmas Carol*. Our Indianapolis Symphony Orchestra puts on amazing shows at an outdoor amphitheater in the summertime, some even with fireworks. And I know it's kind of creepy, but how can you not love *The Phantom of the Opera*?

4. Go out for breakfast before church. Then, after your church celebration, ask a prayer minister to pray with you over your relationship. If this isn't offered at your church on a regular basis, then ask a trusted friend or relative to pray with you for the relationship.

5. Learn something new together like ballroom dancing. Dress in formal attire for this one. The next time you attend a friend's wedding or a school dance, you'll have something special for the dance floor.

6. Take a day trip to a nearby city and explore its museums or downtown shops. Buy a souvenir to remember the adventure together. If you make a habit of this one, you could start a scrapbook to save those memories.

7. Try fishing together. If you don't want to touch the slimy worms, hot dogs may do the trick. While you're waiting for the fish to bite do a little exercise together

to exchange affirmations. Each of you can make a list of reasons why your sweetie is important to you. Write down everything you can think of that you admire about his or her character. This is so important and is a contrast to premarital relationships with sexual intimacy which often focus on outward appearances. You each need to know you are loved for who you are and who God made you to be. Nurture and encourage the uniqueness you see in each other.

8.   If you live in a river town consider a ferry boat cruise. I know it's expensive but it's a great way to lavish on your honey.

Sweet Gestures

"How handsome you are, my beloved!
Oh, how charming!
And our bed is verdant." Song of Songs 1:16

Okay, so you can't express your love for each other in the same way since your commitment to purity. You'll just have to get creative with showing affection. In the past, you may have embraced and kissed each other, which often led to other things. Now when you feel strong feelings for one another, you will have to verbalize it without groping. This can actually be more meaningful. Don't limit yourself to what you can do or say during dates together, but start doing things behind the scenes through sweet gestures. This shows your loved one that you're thinking of him or her while you're apart. It also shows that you are sensitive to his or her feelings and needs.

Here are some ideas for starters:

1. Secretly give your honey's car a makeover inside and out with a good car wash and wax, and even vacuum the interior. Then leave a flower or love note on the dash as a sign that you were there.

2. Bring a bouquet of flowers or just one single exotically beautiful flower. This can be at the start of a date or just on a random occasion.

3. Find a $5.00 gift or a fast food gift card and leave it where your sweetie will find it.

4. Speak words of praise into his or her heart and spirit. This can be more meaningful when done in the presence of friends or family members. Be his or her biggest fan, both in public and in private.

5. Listen to each other and learn to communicate clearly. This is the best gift you can give. You might need to read between the lines and go beyond the words a person is using, but also hear what his emotions are conveying.

6. Pay attention when your mate is going through a stressful time and find a way to help bear their burden or make their load a little lighter. Lower the expectations you have of one another.

7. Give each other a mulligan. In other words… give a do-over. Overlook an offense. Be a grace giver. Choose to forgive a word spoken in emotion, and believe in the heart of your partner.

Seven

Purity After a Broken Marriage or Relationship

"...He has sent me to... comfort all who mourn, and provide for those who grieve in Zion—to bestow on them a crown of beauty instead of ashes, the oil of joy instead of mourning, and a garment of praise instead of a spirit of despair."
Isaiah 61:1-3

I am convinced that no one walks down the aisle and proclaims their wedding vows while thinking, "I hope this works out. If not, I guess I'll find someone else." We might have cold feet or some fear tucked away in our hearts about the marriage's future. We might have a list of contingencies in our minds such as, "As long as he doesn't cheat on me," or "As long as she supports my career path." But most of us think it will really work out and hope for a "happily ever after" end to the story.

Sometimes it simply doesn't work out that way. For many of you, the story was no fairytale. Let me just say, NO ONE has the fairytale. Marriage is *work*! After 17 years with my husband, I can testify to that fact. Each person brings a different set of expectations, hopes, and dreams to the marriage, and tries to work out their differences while loving and respecting each other …we hope.

Ephesians 5:21 calls us to *"Submit to one another out of reverence for Christ."* Then, more specifically, wives are told to *"submit yourselves to your own husbands as you do to the Lord…"* Husbands are instructed to *"love your wives, just as Christ loved the church and gave himself up for her…"* How fabulous our marriage relationships would be if we were able to follow this guidance perfectly. But this is far from easy and is *so* against our human nature. We want our own way and we are easily offended. We add up hurt after hurt and we eventually fail to see one another as precious. Our spouse becomes our enemy and those beautiful vows we spoke so eloquently at the altar become a faint memory.

In their wonderful book, <u>Made To Be Loved, Enjoying Spiritual Intimacy with God and Your Spouse (1999)</u>, Steve and Valerie Bell describe the normal stage that a marriage relationship goes through as their youthful love dies but gives way to a more mature kind of love. But many relationships don't survive this very difficult transition and the cost becomes too great. "Life that was meant to be celebrated in relationship together becomes a practice in enduring. For the investment of your entire lifetime, too often the return is meager affection overshadowed by disillusionment and disappointment. No one who is truly honest would blame someone in this kind of marriage for sometimes thinking, "*There has to be more*'" (p. 25).

Some of you tried so hard to save that marriage, but for whatever reason, the relationship died. Maybe it wasn't even your choice. Maybe your spouse refused to work through the issues with you. Maybe you made some mistakes and the damage felt irreparable. Maybe you both just grew exhausted of trying, or were so wounded you couldn't pick yourself up and go on. Maybe the realization that you no longer had feelings of love for your spouse, or that they no longer had feelings of love for you, was so painful you couldn't bear it any longer. Not only have you grieved and mourned over the death of a dream, you may have bitterness over the hurt inflicted, and you've battled over the house, things, and even children in court.

Jesus was the fulfillment of that prophesy cited above in Isaiah 61. Luke 4:17-21 tells us that at the synagogue He unrolled the scroll of Isaiah and chose this scripture to read: *"The Spirit of the Lord is on me, because he has anointed me to preach good news to the poor. He has sent me to proclaim freedom for the prisoners and recovery of sight for the blind, to release the oppressed, to proclaim the year of the Lord's favor."* Then he said to the crowd, *"Today this scripture is fulfilled in your hearing."* I encourage you to read the entire passage in Isaiah 61 that Jesus was referencing.

I say all this to remind you that Jesus is Healer of the brokenhearted and He comforts those who mourn. He wants to replace your ashes with beauty because it displays the splendor of God in your life. The fact you're reading this book tells me that, no matter what mistakes you made in past relationships, this time you're trying to do it right. You want that new beginning for this current relationship. Maybe you didn't know about

God's pattern for marriage the first time around and you see this new relationship as a second chance. Dating, now, is more serious than ever for you because you have felt the weight of a marriage gone wrong. What does dating now look like for you?

The temptations to cross the safety of physical purity may be stronger because you've been accustomed to physical intimacy in a marriage. The ache of loneliness may be more pronounced because you have had that partner by your side. On the other hand, you may approach a new dating relationship more guarded emotionally, because of a fear of being hurt again.

We have several friends who have gone through this experience. They have lived through a broken marriage and tried to pick up the pieces and go on. Each of these couples have placed God first in their relationship and tried to model their second marriage as described in Ephesians. I asked each of them, "What was the dating period like? How did you try to remain pure since you'd already experienced an intimate marriage relationship? What were some challenges you faced and how did you overcome them?" My girlfriends were able to share with me that, while they didn't always overcome the temptations perfectly, they tried to avoid situations that would become a snare, such as being alone at one another's apartment or house too late at night. They had godly friends that were able to hold them accountable. They kept coming back to God for strength and guidance.

Purity is so much more than refraining from physical temptations. According to the dictionary, purity means "lack of guilt or evil thoughts" (Merriam-Webster's Dictionary). The synonyms listed are "chasteness, immaculacy, innocence, modesty, and chastity." This is a picture of being perfectly clean, avoiding any sexual acts outside of marriage, and being free from vanity.

You may be saying, "Laura how can I be perfectly clean and free from vanity?" That's exactly how I felt, after trying to reclaim purity in my dating relationship. I had already blown it. Also, though I had never been married before, I was in serious relationships that I watched crumble to the ground. The temptation to think more lowly of myself or more highly of myself than I ought is always there. I am reminded of another verse from Isaiah 1:18, *"Come now, let us settle the matter," says the Lord. "Though your sins are like scarlet, they shall be as white as snow; though they are red as crimson, they shall be like wool."* It is He that purifies us, by the sacrifice of Jesus. We receive His righteousness, and one that we cannot earn. We therefore cannot take the credit. He gets all the glory. Though we still have choices to make.

As mentioned before, Psalm 119:9 says, *"How can a young person stay on the path of purity? By living according to your word."* Striving to live a life of purity means that we learn God's standards through reading the Bible and then we obey them. We don't give into our flesh, which means essentially living for ourselves and our desires. We submit our lives to God and do what we believe is pleasing to Him.

Why do we go through all this effort? Hasn't Jesus already forgiven our sins, past, present and future? It is out of our gratitude to a loving, gracious God who went to such great lengths for that forgiveness. Also, if we persevere, we will have a testimony for future generations, as we share our story, and they see the way God replaces the brokenness in our lives with something marvelous. Submitting, both to God and what He asks us to do, allows that process to happen.

Eight

Engagement

*"You have stolen my heart, my sister, my bride;
you have stolen my heart with one glance of your
eyes, with one jewel of your necklace... You are
a garden locked up, my sister, my bride; you are
a spring enclosed, a sealed fountain." Song of
Solomon 4:9, 12*

Ah, I remember this season. How I longed for this time in our dating relationship. I wanted to hear the words of commitment from him: "Laura, will you marry me?" I wanted to be at a place where I could say with certainty, and wholeheartedly, "Yes, Brian I would love to marry you!" tears and all. The months and years prior to our engagement were trying on us emotionally as we weighed this very important life decision. Daily I would prayerfully ask God if Brian was the one He had for me. "If he's not," I prayed to God, "give me a big slap in the face," because I believed that's what I'd need to walk away from him. As I mentioned before, the only clear answer I felt I ever received from God on this matter was, "Just wait, and watch what I do with him."

Once I derailed Brian's engagement plans when I told him, "I don't think I could make a commitment to you for life before you make a commitment to Jesus." I dropped this line in the middle of a casual conversation. I didn't know Brian already had plans to propose. Apparently he had it all orchestrated, complete with the picnic lunch and even horseback riding at the summer camp where he had been working. I imagine he pictured us riding off into the sunset as a newly engaged couple. But he knew that he hadn't made that very important decision of committing his life to Christ. He wasn't ready, and therefore I couldn't feel comfortable saying yes to him.

A tough lesson for me to learn was that I couldn't be the mediator between Brian and God. I tried that role for so long. Full of enthusiasm, I would share with Brian the experiences and revelations that I was having with Jesus, hoping that he would share my excitement and be spurred on. He listened intently but had very little to say.

It wasn't until I stepped out of the way that Brian was able to meet God face to face. I stopped trying so hard and questioning him. After that Billy Graham Crusade moment I did try to step down and watched things slowly change. He eventually joined a Bible study with other college guys. He began consistently going to church with me. He purchased his own Study Bible and began reading on his own. The signs of change were subtle at first but unmistakable. He began to drop lines in our conversations that hinted at a holy wisdom that I had never heard from him before. I began to see in him the desire to grow with God, which was a prerequisite to being my spiritual leader one day. I finally resolved in my heart, with complete peace and confidence, that I could say "Yes!" should he ever ask for my hand in marriage.

The Question

Then I waited, and waited, and waited. Brian assured me he was only waiting for the right timing. I asked him never to pop the question on a holiday or anniversary because I'd be sure to expect it. Then I waited, and waited, and waited some more. Any date together that was out of the ordinary was suspect. I studied his every move. I fought feelings of disappointment when nothing happened. While I couldn't see it at the time, I now realize that something wonderful *was* happening as he courted me. We continued to grow relationally without the draw of our physical desires. We each were getting better at self-control.

Then, it finally happened. December 31, 1999 was not a day I suspected since I told him never to propose on a holiday. He didn't give me a Christmas gift that year so when he came to my parents' house carrying a large, 2 foot, square box I was filled with anticipation. He was making up for it. He was a sweet guy and I thought a late Christmas present was better than no present at all. He asked if we could open it in my bedroom. I couldn't imagine what he might have bought me of this magnitude. I sat the large cardboard box on my bed and began disassembling it.

Strangely, inside that box was a smaller box, then a smaller box, and another... He always had a sense of humor. As the boxes got smaller and smaller I became more excited as I figured out what he was up to. I finally got to the ring box. When I opened it I found, not a ring, but a small note that said, "Look behind you." I turned around and, behind me, he was on one knee holding out the ring and sweating like a horse. He said, "Laura, will you marry me?" With confidence and love I said, "Yes!"

I asked him if he was nervous or afraid that I wouldn't say yes. He admitted that no, rather, he got the ring stuck on his little finger at his house and just managed to pry it off as I was tearing through the succession of boxes. We celebrated the moment with my family as we went out for dinner to an Italian restaurant in downtown Indianapolis, and brought in the New Year, the new millennium, and our new future.

As we returned to school after the holiday break, Brian's friends teased me, saying, "Laura, why are you marrying Mayer?" That's what they called him. "Because," I answered, "he is my constant source of entertainment." Of course there is more to the story than that, but I still use that phrase to describe him today.

Oh, how I wish you could meet this man. He truly has entertained me and everyone around him for years. He keeps people smiling, always has something positive or funny to say, and doesn't hold a grudge. Yet, at the same time, he cynically has no expectations of others so he doesn't get disappointed. He will spend days working out the Thanksgiving Day crossword puzzle in the paper. And he irritates me with his coupon clipping. But I digress.

The Distance

We picked the date for our wedding to be in June just after our senior year of college. I wouldn't recommend a 17-month engagement because it seems like it will never end. It was beneficial to us because I wanted to finish school first. We didn't foresee it at the time but we would be geographically separated for the last 13 months of our engagement.

I began to feel God's leading to work at a summer camp in Colorado through the Navigators' Ministry in 2000. I knew that it would be my last chance to have an adventure of this kind on my own with God prior to getting married. I was a little nervous to talk to Brian about this idea because in the past, I had been so stingy with my summer time with him. I had struggled with his choices to work at a summer camp just 45 mins away and here I was wanting to go to Colorado without him. As I sheepishly told him of my idea, a smile grew across his face and he laughed at the irony. He gave his full support and said I should apply for the position. With his blessing, I pushed through some fear and, to my amazement, was offered the position of working in the office at a camp in the mountains, mentoring two high school students in their Christian walks. My parents were not so sure about this decision. Mom was looking forward to spending some mother-daughter time together, planning our wedding over that summer vacation. She was concerned about how the time apart would impact mine and Brian's relationship. Dad wondered if the low wages of my summer would cripple us financially as we embarked on our married life together. While there was much to be cautious and concerned about, I could not deny the overwhelming sense I had that God was calling me to Himself for this adventure. I didn't want to say "no" to Him. Off I went.

Eagle Lake Camp was like spiritual boot camp for me. I was trained further in how to lead a small Bible Study, and how to mentor girls one on one. I had more time for solitude than I ever anticipated. I had sweet walks around the lake with Jesus, and sensed His presence with me. I was stripped of my material possessions as I lived out of a trunk for three months. The most valuable lesson I learned was seeing that I could depend fully on God for meeting my emotional needs. I knew that I would miss Brian (and I did), but I wasn't pining after him. I felt content with God's presence. Prior to that summer, it wasn't enough for Brian to tell me that he loved me… I needed to know, "But why, what do you love about me and how much?" I was so insecure. At Eagle Lake I learned to fully rely on God for that love that I so desperately craved. I received that love and was freer to love Brian and others without needing so much validation from them. This would be so vital as we entered a married union together the following year.

During that time God refined both of us in more ways than I can count. Brian took a full-time job in our hometown of Indianapolis, Indiana, that summer. We mailed each other letters and had one phone call each week on my Saturdays off. During a phone conversation towards the end of the summer, Brian told me that he had been praying about a decision to keep his summer job and to transfer to a community college in Indianapolis. I had one more year to finish my Occupational Therapy degree in Cincinnati, Ohio, where we both had previously attended school. We would be two hours apart. This was not what I wanted to hear because I was looking forward to being together again after our summer of separation. But I was happy that for the first time he was seeking God's direction for a major decision. I had to trust that God would lead him and I vowed to support him.

Though difficult, separation during that last year of dating helped us to press on in our desire to remain pure until our wedding day. It would have been easy to rationalize giving in to the physical temptations since we were engaged now. But we weren't married yet. At that point in our lives, we both wanted to walk down the aisle with a clear conscience. I wanted to experience, as much as possible, the innocence God intended for me on that day. I wanted that legacy for my future children.

And more than that, God was still my first Love and I wanted to give Him that gift of obedience out of a pure heart. I truly believe that God blessed and honored these decisions and intentions.

So what should this time of engagement look like for you? Well it's a beautiful season in your relationship as you plan to celebrate your love for each other with all your family and friends. I encourage you to honor God by continuing to live in separate places. Remember that King Solomon praised the Shulamite woman for her virginity and purity, *"You have stolen my heart, my sister, my bride; you have stolen my heart with one glance of your eyes, with one jewel of your necklace... You are a garden locked up, my sister, my bride; you are a spring enclosed, a sealed fountain"* (Song of Solomon 4:9, 12).

Engagement is an opportune time to verbally affirm your future spouse. Brian couldn't show his love or desire for me in physical ways, but he could remind me verbally that I was the only one for him. We appreciated the *"garden locked up... a spring enclosed, a sealed fountain."* These word images refer to the purity of the bride in the passage above. They imply that there is something beautiful and life-giving waiting behind lock and key. That key was mine to give; it was never his to take. We awaited with sweet anticipation the season when we could enjoy all that God had for us in marriage. Brian came to respect his role to protect the gates of my purity. However, along with that, his words of affirmation became even more important to me to assure me of his devotion and commitment.

The Little Foxes

"My dove,... show me your face, let me hear your voice; for your voice is sweet, and your face is lovely. Catch for us the foxes,

the little foxes that ruin the vineyards, our vineyards that are in bloom" (Song of Sol. 2:14-15). The little foxes in this passage are thought to refer to the troubles in our relationships; the annoyances, differences, or grievances. I believe it was by God's design that I didn't find out about our biggest little fox until entering the committed state of our engagement, lest I see it as that slap in the face I mentioned earlier.

It came about quite innocently, as I poured out my feelings to Brian one day, frustrated over giving into food which was an area of sin in my life. I was disappointed with myself because I had 12-stepped this addiction and knew what I needed to do to overcome it. Instead of stopping when I was full that day, I continued eating beyond where I knew my limit should be. Brian comforted me by saying that everyone has a sin issue in their lives, whether it's food, lust, gambling, or something else. In that moment it occurred to me that Brian had never admitted any area of sin to me. He always had it all together, aside from taking extra time to catch up to some of my moral convictions.

I asked quietly, "So what is your issue?" He was silent. He seemed to be afraid to share what was in his heart. How could he comfort me while denying the temptation of sin in his own life? It was one of those moments that happened in slow motion. He said rather sheepishly, "I don't want to talk about it." He had backed himself into a corner. I wanted desperately to know yet was terrified to find out. I saw the vulnerability in his eyes and knew he feared my judgment.

I gently asked, "Is it one of the three things you mentioned?" I said this, knowing it wasn't food, and most likely not gambling either. The only one left was one of my greatest fears: lust. He'd been caught and couldn't deny it. He shook his head "yes." A storm brewed within my heart. I was appalled, angry, and felt betrayed, and yet I had just shown my own vulnerability to my sin of overeating. I knew that his sin of lust, however deep, was no worse than my own 5-year struggle with food addiction, for which he always had shown me compassion and grace.

I listened as he shared his struggle with pornography. Up until that point he hadn't thought it a problem as long as I didn't know. As he waited for me to respond, I thought back to times when I had found him in his dorm room, sleeping through his first class of the day because he had been up late into the night. I recalled times he didn't seem to be where he told me he would be, but gave me a little white lie to paint the picture he thought I wanted to hear. In our four years of dating he had concealed this secret and I had been blind. I held back my anger but I did cry. I expressed to him how it hurt me to know he looked elsewhere for sexual fulfillment. I had believed he was attracted to me, but all at once I felt I wasn't enough. He apologized and vowed to stop, saying it had nothing to do with me or what I couldn't give him at the time. This was hard for me to accept and believe, but I resisted the urge to pass judgment.

Concerning this habit, I asked that he be honest and not lie to me in the future. I knew this would only be possible if I remained approachable and withheld my anger. He reluctantly agreed to my terms as I vowed to not meet his confessions with anger. I depended on him for accountability when it came to food and I wanted for him to be able to count on me for accountability as well. This was the beginning. After he left that night, I cried out to God. I was so confused and afraid. How could I trust him again? How could I enter this commitment of marriage with him and trust in his faithfulness? I begged God, "Please, it has to be gone before we get married."

God had so much to teach both of us. He tenderly told me that my response to Brian's sin should follow God's response to mine. God doesn't meet my confessions with anger, but I believe with sadness and grief. Proverbs 28:13 states, "*Whoever conceals their sins does not prosper, but the one who confesses and renounces them finds mercy.*" The Holy Spirit gently convicts; He doesn't condemn. In Romans 8:1 Paul says, "*Therefore, there is now no condemnation for those who are in Christ Jesus, because through Christ Jesus the law of the Spirit who gives life has set you free from the law of sin and death.*" He gives me undeserved grace.

We were both tested in so many ways. Brian learned that his draw to pornography was more powerful than he realized. When I asked if he had been faithful to me, I learned to trust him when he said "Yes." He learned to trust that I wouldn't become angry when he had to say "No." I learned to meet that honesty with sadness and grace, instead of outrage. I explained how his actions caused me pain. He responded with an acknowledgement and an apology. He eventually found other men to hold him accountable and the slip ups gradually diminished.

As painful as this process was, and as long as it took before we felt freedom from its grip, I have come to appreciate that it caused Brian to fall to his knees before God. For the first time he saw that he needed God...not only for forgiveness, but for His ongoing help. As God healed Brian's life, He also healed my insecurities and brought healing to our relationship as well. Our quest for purity took on a new form as we surrendered these areas to God. It was not just the pursuit of purity together, but the pursuit of purity in our individual lives and thoughts.

I encourage you to ask God to reveal the "little foxes" in your relationship. What is it that He needs to work out between you? Remember, the warning was that the foxes ruin the vineyard in bloom. Be vulnerable with each other and come humbly before

God. Allow Him to reveal the things, large and small, that will be harmful to your relationship. Have hope in the God who is the master of changed lives. If you allow Him access to your heart, He will mold you into the image of His Son, Jesus.

This time of engagement can be a sweet time with you and the Lord as He continues to refine you into the man or woman he intends you to become. That process continues throughout your lifetime. This is a good time to evaluate if there are any desires God has placed in your heart that would be best to pursue before you begin a marriage.

As I mentioned earlier, I attended Eagle Lake Camp in Colorado during the summer prior to our wedding. People thought I was crazy for leaving my fiancé for so long instead of using the summer to plan our wedding and spend time together. It wasn't easy to leave him, but I knew it was my last chance to venture out into the world with God by myself. It was like my honeymoon with God and it was an incredible, life-changing experience. Thankfully, Brian was in full support of this decision.

This leads me to another point. I believe engagement is a time for learning to make decisions together. It's good practice for your future marriage. You can't think of only yourself any longer. Through your marriage, God will make the two of you become one. Planning for your wedding day provides multiple opportunities to exercise decision-making together. You must learn that no decision or issue is more important than the heart of your spouse. The heart of your spouse is a treasure God has entrusted you with. You will answer to God one day according to how you treat one another. I still pray for God's help to show my husband love and grace as we continue to make decisions together in life.

After experiencing several years of marriage, three children, and a few pets later, the wedding ceremonies I have graciously been invited to hold new meaning. I enjoy seeing splashes of the bride and groom's personalities and styles reflected in the ceremony, the song choices, and the decorations. I enjoy celebrating their union, vowing to support them, and watching the gleams in their eyes during their first dance. But in my heart, I pray they learn to rely on God through the joys and the struggles ahead. I recall the time I walked down the aisle myself, with every detail in place. I remember the sweetness of those times with fewer distractions and responsibilities. We were naïve. We didn't know what lay ahead but just knew we would finally be together. We had so much to learn about the kind of love that will last.

Steve and Valerie Bell (1999) speak of these things in <u>Made to be Loved; Enjoying Spiritual Intimacy with God and Your Spouse.</u> They've been married for 28 years and have 25 years of experience ministering to couples. They stress the importance of not relying on our limited ability to love one another, but to seek spiritual intimacy with God as we seek it with each other.

They write, "Our human love, we sadly realized, would not be enough to fulfill, satisfy, and care for each other in the days ahead" (p. 24). Brian and I have experienced this as well. When people ask why we have such a great marriage, we are not able to take the credit. In and of ourselves we cannot make each other happy. We are two selfish creatures who each want our own way if we were to admit it. Our joy in this union comes through the power of the Holy Spirit working in our lives as we each try to submit to God and His plans for us. We each must be acutely aware of the depth of the love of God for us and our spouse. As forgiven followers of Christ we are able to love one another in a more complete and fulfilling way.

Begin relying on God now for every aspect of your lives, your relationship, and even your wedding day. Admit that you need Him. As human beings, we are afraid to admit our weaknesses; we're embarrassed for others to see we don't have it all together. Yet, to admit to God that we can't do life without Him is to invite the power of His presence. When we finally let go of the reigns, God can steer.

In the months before your big day, as you meet with the florist, the photographer, the caterer, the baker and the candlestick maker, the prayer of your heart could be, "God help us bring glory and honor to you through our wedding." As the world wants to make that day "all about us," God's people have an opportunity to make the day "all about what God has done in our lives."

We had this in mind as we carefully selected each reading and each song for the ceremony. One of our party favors dispensed to our guests was a CD including some of our favorite Christian songs that many of our friends or family members may not have been exposed to. Prior to the pictures that morning, we had a moment at the altar together in which we exchanged letters of how we felt about the day. A mentor of mine prayed over me and my bridesmaids in the dressing room before everything began. I had a peace and a calm that sustained me through the hiccups in the day that didn't go as planned. I believe that on June 2, 2001, we displayed not only who we were as a couple, but who God is to our guests.

Nine

Rocky Roads

"It is better to take refuge in the Lord than to trust in man. It is better to take refuge in the Lord than to trust in princes." Psalm 118:8-9

I f you haven't had rocky roads in the past, I assure you they are inevitable in your future. You and your partner are two imperfect people with different goals, different expectations, and different ideas on how to resolve conflicts. In the heat of the moment, it's hard to focus on his dreamy eyes, her soothing voice, or any of the other things that initially drew you together. Are you able to work through your conflicts and differences and move toward oneness? That has certainly been a challenge over the years for Brian and me. I must say that now our challenges do draw us together and help us to deepen our unity. However, early in our relationship, those differences were frustrations that really threatened our commitment to one another.

So what if it just isn't working out? What if you decide in your heart this relationship may not lead to marriage? One of you just doesn't have peace about it. I want to be sensitive to your situation because it is not an easy place to be. I have been in other dating relationships that dissolved; the longest one lasted over a year. Don't laugh… it was long to a high school sophomore. "Dissolve" isn't the right word because in each of those early relationships we had to be emotionally teased apart. We couldn't just walk away from one another. It was a process of convincing myself that while I still had feelings for him, our relationship was not ultimately what I wanted. My hopes and dreams for my future were tied to those relationships. I probably had names picked out for our children.

Brian and I even had a couple moments, while dating, when our relationship teetered on the edge of existence. The first was during our senior year of high school. We had a plan to attend the same college. That was a calculated move for us to be together. We both were looking forward to the future. However, I became insecure about the next season in our lives. I convinced myself that other girls there would catch his attention. I knew he liked me, and said he loved me. But I doubted the depth of his devotion to me. Would it withstand the excitement of the adventure ahead? As we talked about the freshman year of college together, and what to expect, I would say, "I can't wait to be able to see you every day, walk to classes together, meet for dinners…" He would say, "I can't wait to meet new people."

I looked for an opportunity to tell him how I was feeling. I had come to my decision and finally I broke the news to him at a park after school. I told him that I was afraid I would hold him back in college, and I felt it best that we go our separate ways. He took it so graciously that I was sure I made the right decision. He didn't even seem to care in the moment and agreed we could still be friends.

A couple of weeks later, a mutual friend told me that Brian was actually upset over this breakup. I wondered if maybe I had made a mistake. I certainly still had feelings for him. But why didn't he fight for me or try harder to keep me?

Soon afterwards, while standing at our lockers, I took a risk and asked, "Why don't we just start over?" He laughed and agreed. Later he admitted that while he felt breaking up was a mistake, he initially took the news from me so easily because he wanted me to be happy and didn't want me to feel bad for breaking up with him. I guess I wanted him to read my mind when I tried to let him off the hook before he could break my heart: "I want you to want me. Don't let me go."

Yet, I wasn't convinced. That summer before college, I was looking forward to spending some time together and solidifying our relationship. Brian decided to take a job as a camp counselor, located 45 minutes away. This devastated me as an 18-year-old. We had only been dating a year, survived a breakup, were about to head off to college, and now I can only see him on weekends? All summer?

He did send me cards and letters each week. He came home to visit and raved about his camp experiences on our dates. He was making an impact on all the kids, connecting with other counselors and enjoying the time in the woods. I was happy for his happiness, but camp seemed to pull him farther and farther away from me. ME. What about ME? What about our life together?

I wrote him a letter and mailed it to camp. Yes, I tried to break up with him in a *letter*. I was releasing him as I felt he just couldn't bring himself to break my heart. Brian remembered his previous experience with me and called right away and fought for me this time. He assured me over the phone that he *did* want to be with me. His love letters and original poetry apparently hadn't been enough for me with my doubts and insecurities. Maybe I had been testing him. I certainly kept that poor boy on his toes.

Can you relate to our experience? You may be older and less hormonal, but still dealing with insecurities. Maybe your honey actually did make the break with you. This is a good time to check the contents of your heart. Where does your devotion lie? Is God truly your First Love? The answers to these questions will help determine how far you fall during hard times.

If your self-worth was tied to this relationship, you are in for some rocky roads ahead. However, if your sense of worth comes from how Jesus sees you, you will not be shaken during trials like theses. He will heal your emotional brokenness over time as you commune with Him. In Revelations 3:20 Jesus says, *"Here I am. I stand at the door and knock. If anyone hears my voice and opens the door, I will come in and eat with him and he with me."*

Jesus is not a traveling salesman trying to get you to buy a religion. He wants to sit down and have a meal with you... to commune with you. He also wants to comfort you. In Zephaniah 3:17 God says, *"The Lord your God is with you. He is mighty to save. He takes great delight in you. He quiets you with His love; He rejoices over you with singing."* He's crazy about you and wants to be your First Love. You only need to open the front door and let Him in.

You see, I used to think that the highest goal in my life was to find that perfect life-mate… someone who would truly love me forever. So anytime a relationship failed the test of time, my sense of security and self-worth unraveled like a fraying rope. Once I realized that Jesus longed to be my First Love, and that I needed Him to have that place in my life, my sense of self-worth was safe in Him. My security for my future was protected by Him.

My earthly relationships were important, but I realized that my relationship with Him was eternal and paramount. He will do His good work in and through me if I allow Him, whether I am single, dating, or married... working or unemployed... a momma or childless, or even an empty nester. My mission is to allow my life, in all its seasons, to adorn the Gospel, showing the world the love and grace of my God (read Titus 2). My self-worth and identity come from the exciting ride of being a Christian, regardless of my circumstances. First and foremost, I am *in Him*.

Jesus loves you and me more than any earthly man or woman ever could. He desires a relationship with you despite your past or present flaws. In fact, the purpose of marriage is to be a reflection of the Father's love for His people. We are to mirror Christ's love for the Church. Like many experiences in life, marriage serves to refine us, purify us if we allow it, changing us slowly over time into the image of Christ. That's why it's so important to hold the marriage vows in high honor. Hebrews 13:4 says, *"Marriage should be honored by all and the marriage bed kept pure, for God will judge the adulterer and all the sexually immoral."*

If you've come to a place where one of you feels you can't make this kind of commitment, it's best not to make the vows. Don't make a vow you can't keep. That being said, there is no perfect mate. Marriage is a *much-grace-required* state of being. It demands ongoing maintenance if it is to last and thrive. Be careful that you're not so focused on the ideal that you reject the real.

How did Brian and I finally move beyond our rocky moments? Well, from my perspective, I believe these moments tested our commitment. Brian showed me that our relationship was so valuable to him that he was willing to make adjustments for me. This attitude has continued through the 17 years of marriage, and I have tried to have the same attitude with him. Once I saw that he had a heart for God, I trusted in God's faithfulness to mold each of us along the way. He had a surrendered spirit. I was convicted to be a grace giver as well as to surrender my areas of pride to God. And let me tell you, that is not a short list. I have learned to stop expecting Brian to read my mind and stop trying to read his. We learned to talk about our feelings and insecurities and give one another the chance to give affirmation. As I kept seeking God and growing in my walk with Him, my relationship with Brian improved.

We answer to a higher authority than just one another. We strive to love and respect one another because we are trying to act in obedience to the Most High God. Our feelings for each other are not dependable. Emotions come and go. It's a *choice* to be committed, out of reverence for our God. In order for a marriage to be successful for the long haul, I believe the qualities that truly matter are an attitude of submission to one another out of submission to God, a mindset of grace and forgiveness, and a sense of appreciation for the heart of one's spouse.

Why such a lowly standing, you might ask? Jesus washed the feet of His disciples and called us to do the same (John 13:1-17). He demonstrated for us an attitude of submission and a servant's heart. He exemplified grace and forgiveness as the disciples missed the heart of His 3-year mission, with eternal implications. He saw past their flaws to their heart and potential, calling Peter the rock on which He would build His church, for example (Matthew 16:18).

Ephesians 5:1-2 says, *"Be imitators of God, therefore, as dearly loved children and live a life of love, just as Christ loved us and gave himself up for us as a fragrant offering and sacrifice to God."* Regardless of where you are in your present earthly relationships, or what you have done in the past, God cares immensely about you. He will weave, if you allow Him, all of your experiences together to make you more and more into the image of Christ over time. The question is: Can you trust Him with your future and your dreams? Will you choose to move forward through the mountains and the valleys, believing that He holds you in the palm of His hand?

Ten

Replacing the Shame and Guilt

"Jesus straightened up and asked her, 'Woman, where are they? Has no one condemned you?'

'No one, Sir,' she said.

'Then neither do I condemn you,' Jesus declared. 'Go now and leave your life of sin.'" John 8:10-11

I n this beautiful account, a woman who was caught in the act of adultery was given new life. Can you imagine the shame and guilt she must've felt as the Pharisees walked in on her romantic encounter, paraded her to the front of the crowd, and exposed her sin? We see no mention of the man involved in this act. I guess they left him behind. Can you imagine the fear that gripped her heart as they picked up stones to kill her? She couldn't deny her guilt and had no defense.

Then, Jesus, who knew the sin in every man and woman's heart wisely said, *"If any one of you is without sin, let him be the first to throw a stone at her"* (John 8:7). He didn't deny the crime or offer excuses for her. He didn't deny the justice that the Law of Moses required. The result: *"At this, those who heard began to go away one at a time, the older ones first, until only Jesus was left, with the woman still standing there"* (verse 9). They came to realize that they all were guilty before God. Not one was without sin. Everyone deserved the same fate and had received mercy. Jesus was the only One who had the right to condemn her, but in His mercy and grace, He lifted her up and gave her a new lease on life.

Paul, in Romans 8:1-2, echoes Jesus' character demonstrated in that story, *"Therefore, there is now no condemnation for those who are in Christ Jesus, because through Christ Jesus the law of the Spirit of life set me free from the law of sin and death."* The key phrase here is: "In Christ." The woman above was caught in the act, proven guilty, and condemned to die. On a different day that might've been her fate. In Christ she was found guilty. But In Christ her accusers were discovered to be no less guilty of sin. However, In Christ she was given a choice—a turning point. She could continue on the same destructive path, or she could choose a redeemed life In Christ, walking in freedom. I wish I could've seen her walk away from Jesus that day with her head held up high. I wonder what changes she made in her life after this encounter and how it impacted those who knew her.

Can you relate at all to this woman? Maybe you were caught in the act of sin, or maybe you hold a secret sin in your heart. Maybe you aren't ready to let the sin go yet. However, this is not an option for us In Christ. I know that for me, in regards to my sexual sin, I spent many years rationalizing it. However, once God convicted my heart, once I was ready to listen to and accept His truth, I had no choice but to change. I felt the sting of shame and guilt brought by my sin.

People don't always react to the shame and guilt in their lives by rationalizing their sin as I did. Often times we simply ignore it. We are afraid to expose our sin before God, knowing our guilt, and fearing His judgment and disappointment in us. We may bury the shame with not so great habits or with excuses. When we ignore or bury the guilt, we still feel dirty and unworthy. This creates a wall between us and God, making us afraid to face Him fully. I don't know about you, but I don't want a wall between me and my Heavenly Father. Nothing on Earth is worth indulging in if it means breaking our relationship with God.

Sometimes we do acknowledge our guilt and shame and try to change with our own strength. When we try to change in our own efforts we are often left frustrated because our strength is insufficient. We can create rules to change our outward appearances, but they won't change our hearts. Just as a strict diet won't eliminate your desire to eat cake, rules won't eliminate your lust. It is only when we vulnerably stand before God, and give our mistakes and weaknesses to Him in prayer, that we can fully change. This change is a process and won't happen overnight. He is the One causing the change in us in His perfect timing.

Haven't you found this to be true? Each time we mess up we need to return and surrender to Him. The difference is that we no longer identify with the shame and guilt, but instead we accept His free gift of forgiveness… each time. Along this journey, our sinful pattern loses its allure for us and our sinful episodes get farther apart. The call of the Holy Spirit in our hearts grows stronger and becomes more attractive to us than the call of sin. Then we can walk in His new light with our heads held up high. I believe this is what it means to be <u>In Christ</u>. 2 Corinthians 5:17 says it so beautifully, *"Therefore, if anyone is in Christ, the new creation has come: The old has gone, the new is here!"* Believe that you *are* a new creation and let your relationship with Him change you from the inside out.

Maybe the shame and guilt you carry in your heart is old, originating from a past relationship. In the Book of Isaiah, God has such a sweet call to His people who had been unfaithful to Him. And let's be honest here; whenever we have given in to any area of sin in our lives, we have actually been unfaithful to our God. I believe these words are a call to us as well.

Isaiah 43:18-19 says: *"Forget the former things; do not dwell on the past. See, I am doing a new thing! Now it springs up; do you not perceive it? I am making a way in the wilderness and streams in the wasteland."* I have always loved that verse. God doesn't want us to keep focusing on our past sins. Instead we need to keep our eyes on Him and on the new thing He is doing in our lives. Do you see the way He is making through your own wilderness? Do you see His fruit springing up in your life? Embrace it and walk in it.

Let your response to this amazing grace and forgiveness of your sinful past be an overflowing of worship to God. I am reminded of the story in Luke 7:36-50 of another sinful woman. Like the lady in John 8, she doesn't even have a name. Read this passage with me.

> *"When one of the Pharisees invited Jesus to have dinner with him, he went to the Pharisee's house and reclined at the table. A woman in that town who lived a sinful life learned that Jesus*

was eating at the Pharisee's house, so she came there with an alabaster jar of perfume. As she stood behind him at his feet weeping, she began to wet his feet with her tears. Then she wiped them with her hair, kissed them and poured perfume on them."

She was obviously repentant over the sins that had colored her past. Look at her brokenness. Look at her courage to enter the house, uninvited, to approach her Savior. They all knew who she was. Were her tears an expression of shame or were they evidence of her overflowing emotions of gratitude to Jesus? As she broke the expensive alabaster jar of perfume, was it a symbol of breaking away from her old life to make Jesus her Lord? I cannot imagine a more humble position than kissing Jesus' feet and wiping them with her hair, which normally would have been covered. What an expression of worship! She was not focused on what the men in the room were thinking or saying of her, but instead fixed her eyes on Jesus.

This caused quite a stir in the room. Let's read on.

"When the Pharisee who had invited him saw this, he said to himself, 'If this man were a prophet, he would know who is touching him and what kind of woman she is—that she is a sinner.'

Jesus answered him, 'Simon, I have something to tell you.'

'Tell me, teacher,' he said.

'Two people owed money to a certain moneylender. One owed him five hundred denarii, and the other fifty. Neither of them had the money to pay him back, so he forgave the

debts of both. Now which of them will love him
more?'

Simon replied, 'I suppose the one who had the
bigger debt forgiven.'

'You have judged correctly,' Jesus said.

Then he turned toward the woman and said
to Simon, 'Do you see this woman? I came into
your house. You did not give me any water for
my feet, but she wet my feet with her tears and
wiped them with her hair. You did not give me
a kiss, but this woman, from the time I entered,
has not stopped kissing my feet. You did not put
oil on my head, but she has poured perfume on
my feet. Therefore, I tell you, her many sins have
been forgiven—as her great love has shown. But
whoever has been forgiven little loves little.'

Then Jesus said to her, 'Your sins are forgiven.'

The other guests began to say among
themselves, 'Who is this who even forgives sins?'

Jesus said to the woman, 'Your faith has saved
you; go in peace'" (Luke 7:39-50).

If you and I truly understand that we have been forgiven for
our past, present, and future sins, then our response should be
an outpouring of love and worship as well. We will be *"the one*
who loved Him more". How great was your debt? Not only have
I placed the idol of sexual immorality before Him in my past,
but I also surrendered an idol of food and dieting. I allowed
anxiety, people pleasing, and approval of man to be louder in
my heart than the truths of God's Word. As I explained earlier, I
developed an eating disorder in my teens that took several years
to break free from. But the good news is He broke me free! I

will be forever grateful to Him for rescuing me from the grips of my selfish sin and I can only hope that I will spend the rest of my days worshipping and loving *my* Savior.

Beyond accepting the gift of grace and forgiveness that Jesus offers to you, as well as the hope of change, you need to offer this free gift to one another. I am reminded of the marriage advice Brian's grandfather, George Mayer, gave us just before we tied the knot, "There's no chimney so clean it don't smoke sometimes." Once I got past the fact he was comparing our relationship to a chimney, I realized what he was saying: Don't expect perfection. Give one another room to make mistakes. Extend grace to one another. If Jesus Himself no longer condemns us, how can we continue to condemn one another? I must say, that over the years, Brian has ministered to my soul more than anyone else in the world, because he has never withheld grace from me. Sure, we've had our share of arguments and hurt feelings. But he never has neglected to forgive me or seek my forgiveness. He has never held a matter over my head, but has given me permission to move on, beyond my shame and guilt.

Our eighteenth year of marriage continues to teach me this lesson. Brian and I are on the same page with most things. That "two becoming one" thing really does happen over time as you submit to God in your lives. We finish each other's sentences from time to time, enjoy the same church, and share similar parenting views as we keep learning together. However, we are still two different people with different personalities, likes, and dislikes.

I am an early riser but also am becoming a night owl. Brian values his sleep. I am task driven and a planner, while he likes spontaneity. My to-do list often overwhelms me, while he feels there will always be things left on the table and they will keep. His coupon clipping drives me crazy and makes me feel pressured to buy things I don't think I need. I have trouble saying "no" to people while he refrains from saying "yes".

I believe God gave us to one another to balance each other out. I have become more laid back over the years, and I believe he has become more organized. We often use our differences to discuss a matter and end up somewhere in the middle together. But some days, when we are both stressed and tired, we get a little, shall we say, snippy with each other? One of us says something that offends the other. Then the offender gets mad that he or she was misunderstood.

We go from expressing our emotions with intense words, maybe a few tears on my side, to slowly calming down and working through the issues. It is hard for me to feel loving towards him when he's offended me. I'm sure he would say the same of me.

But ultimately we serve a great God who has cancelled all of our debts. And He tells us to love one another and submit to one another, regardless of whether we are in the right, or on the defensive. We are not to go to bed angry. Ephesians 4:26 says, *"'In your anger do not sin': Do not let the sun go down while you are still angry."* We always work it out, hug, and drop the matter the next day. In doing so, we extend grace to one another and believe in the goodness of our spouse's heart.

Eleven

Moving From Hedonism to Godliness

"Love is patient, love is kind. It does not envy, it does not boast, it is not proud. It is not rude, it is not self-seeking, it is not easily angered, it keeps no record of wrongs. Love does not delight in evil but rejoices with the truth. It always protects, always trusts, always hopes, always perseveres. Love never fails." 1 Corinthians 13:4-8

As I write this, Brian and I are spending a long weekend together in Florida to celebrate our anniversary. We spent a little time at the happiest place on Earth, Walt Disney World. Everywhere you look there are reminders of the fairytale dreams of finding true love and a "happily ever after" ending to the story. As a little girl, I definitely had the princess complex. I watched the movies of Cinderella, Belle, and Sleeping Beauty, and wanted to be like these beautiful creatures. I longed for the day when some Prince Charming would see something beautiful in me and whisk me away for our own happily ever after. In these lovely stories, true love always won. It was an irresistible force.

As I grew older, I suppose the cynical side of Hollywood crept into my view. I saw stories of a couple's "happily ever after" become dashed to pieces on the shores of reality. I looked around and saw families of my friends or classmates broken apart by divorce. Worry entered dreams for my own future. I entertained fears of my own Prince Charming falling out of love with me one day.

As a child, I frequently was complimented on my pretty eyes, my hair, or my figure; but what if, as I grew older, I wouldn't maintain all of these features? My dreams turned into fears. I feared falling out of love, losing my beauty, and the ultimate disappointment and failure in my mind—divorce.

As I approached my dating years, I believe my hopes and dreams, combined with my fears, caused me to place a wall around my heart. This contributed to many of the rocky roads that Brian and I faced while dating. However, as we have transitioned into marriage ourselves, through the years God has taught me so much along the way, concerning *His* view for our future. I no longer had to live in fear, and as I learned to trust in God and His goodness, the walls began to come down.

As I choose wedding cards for family and friends now, I steer clear of the rosy sentiments promising the bride and groom their happily ever after. Instead, I look for cards that tell them, as wonderful as this day is, the road will not be easy and will take dedicated hard work. The beauty in their future life together will come through submitting to God, relying on His help, and continually making the choice to love one another through the good times and the bad. I would say the same to you.

You see, the problem with placing "happily ever after" as the goal for our future, is that it's so selfish. It is human. Don't we all just want to be happy? We instinctively live for our own happiness. Instead, as Christians, our aim should be to live for God and to seek His will in our lives and His glory. The beautiful thing is that as we set our sights on living for Him and not for ourselves, we in turn will find His blessing in our lives. We aren't just sacrificing our happiness, we are removing it from the altar.

I love what David has to say in Psalm 34:

"I will extol the Lord at all times; his praise will always be on my lips. My soul will boast in the Lord; let the afflicted hear and rejoice. Glorify the Lord with me; let us exalt his name together. I sought the Lord, and he answered me; he delivered me from all my fears. Those who look to him are radiant, their faces are never covered with shame. This poor man called, and the Lord heard him; he saved him out of all his troubles. The angel of the Lord encamps around those who fear him, and he delivers them. Taste and see that the Lord is good; blessed is the man who takes refuge in him. Fear the Lord, you his saints, for those who fear him lack nothing. The lions may grow weak and hungry, but those who seek the Lord lack no good thing…"

David had such a beautiful, real relationship with the Lord. His heart overflowed with praises of God's goodness and love to him. He gave God credit for delivering him from trouble. He gave God credit for the good things in his life. He was not living merely for his own happiness, but sought to follow God and to bring glory to His name. When we take time to read through the Book of Psalms, which is kind of like David's prayer journal, we can't help but be swept up with the emotions of gratitude and love he expressed to God in response to His faithfulness and goodness. We see God's forgiveness to David when he made mistakes. We see His righteous judgment and His incomprehensible grace through David's eyes.

Marriage can be a canvas for displaying these wonderful qualities of God as well. This is a much higher aim than our own "happily ever after." God used a marriage, in the book of Hosea, to teach Israel a valuable lesson about His relationship with His people. In this story, which transpired in 8th century B.C., God asked the prophet, Hosea, to take an adulterous woman as his wife. She had children with Hosea but then left him for another man and later became a prostitute. God instructed Hosea in Chapter 3:1

"Go, show your love to your wife again, though she is loved by another and is an adulteress. Love her as the Lord loves the Israelites, though they turn to other gods and love the sacred raisin cakes."

Why did God ask Hosea to go through all of the heartache and take her back? He had every right to toss her aside after what she did to him. It was a picture to show Israel how much God loved His people. He wanted them to know that even though they had been unfaithful like Hosea's wife, and deserved to be tossed aside, He would still love them and take them back. Always.

Hosea bought his wife back and was reconciled to her. I imagine he didn't "fall in love" with her again, but *chose* to love her as God instructed. While Hosea's situation was both unique and intense, when we choose to love our spouse while he or she is undeserving, and offer forgiveness for wrongs, we are demonstrating the gracious love and mercy of our Heavenly Father.

The disciple John wrote, in the book of Revelation, about the Church being the Bride of Christ. In chapter 19:6-8 he wrote:

"Then I heard what sounded like a great multitude, like the roar of rushing waters and like loud peals of thunder, shouting: 'Hallelujah! For our Lord God Almighty reigns. Let us rejoice and be glad and give him glory! For the wedding of the Lamb has come, and his bride has made herself ready. Fine linen, bright and clean, was given her to wear.' (Fine linen stands for the righteous acts of the saints.)"

Marriage is a platform for displaying a profound mystery, as we have begun to explore in Ephesians 5. The pattern God gives us for husbands and wives is a reflection of Christ loving His bride, the Church. Husbands are to love their wives as Christ loved the Church, even laying down His life. Wives are to submit to their husbands and honor them as heads of their households, just as the Church submits to Christ and honors Him as the Head of the Body of Christ. We are to be united together as one flesh, as the Church is united with Christ and becomes one body. This mutual love and respect creates a special unity within a marriage that brings honor to God and displays His glory. It is a sacrificial type of love and respect and is not possible if we are only seeking our own happiness in life.

The kind of love described at the beginning of this chapter in 1 Corinthians 13, which is often used at wedding ceremonies, is what we as Christians are called to. If we truly love others, we will be patient with one another when it's undeserved, as Jesus is patient with us. We will be kind with our words and actions, as Jesus is kind to us. We won't be envious or jealous towards each other. We won't be boastful, thinking our role is more important or that we know better. We won't be rude when we are frustrated or don't get our way. We won't be self-seeking. It's counter-cultural to put our spouse first, but isn't that what God is calling us to? If we truly love like our Heavenly Father we will not be easily angered, but slow to anger, keeping no record of wrongs. True Christian love does not delight in evil (enjoying being proved right over our spouse) but rejoices with the truth. It always protects, always trusts and hopes, always perseveres. This kind of love can't fail because it is heavenly.

Shift

It's a tall order to demand that our marriage relationship reflect the union of Jesus and His beloved Church. How do we live for His honor and not just our own happiness? We need to shift our positions sometimes and move toward one another. What does that look like in real life? Here is an example from my marriage.

Brian and I are learning to let go of our own desires sometimes and make little sacrifices in order to do life together. I love to plan ahead… way ahead. I have a tendency to fill our family agenda with a host of activities. I like to go and do things, get out of the house and escape the mundane list of never ending chores. I have numerous interests and want to get the most out of every square inch of life.

Brian is a homebody. He is spontaneous. He loves to have space to be home and relax, to sleep in, and to have time to work around the house and yard. Then, on a whim, he may decide to whisk the kids off to a state park for some hiking and creek stomping. That would all be well and good with me… as long as it was scheduled.

My schedule makes me feel secure, and free unclaimed time makes me feel like I'm failing. In other words, I feel like I'm not being productive and I'm missing out on an opportunity. Time is so precious and I see it slipping through my fingers. We both had to move toward one another in this issue. If I always sought my own way on the agenda, my husband would feel out of control of his life and grow resentful. If he never let me plan our weekends, I would be full of anxiety and feel lost and overwhelmed in the to-do list of my mind. We have to work at this together out of love and respect for one another. I now try to consult him before I write things down on the calendar. Then I try to leave some empty space to allow him the spontaneity that he needs.

We have learned to move beyond our initial irritation with one another and to appreciate and even be amused by our differences. We allow ourselves to shift our thinking and be molded together in unity. In working through these conflicts and differences, we have the opportunity to give one another grace and love, and in doing so we bring glory to our Heavenly Father. It is the Holy Spirit living and working in and through us that allows us to see one another through His eyes and set aside our own desires in order to bless one another.

Submit

God has asked me to respect my husband and submit to him, even when I don't agree with his decisions. That's hard. Sometimes I have to restrain my desire to be right in a situation and lean on Brian's leadership instead. God has proven repeatedly that He is sovereign, He is guiding my husband, and I can trust in that leadership, even when it doesn't make sense to me.

Here is an example from our life. Because I work in Home Healthcare, I drove over 140,000 miles with my vehicle in seven years. We realized it was time to replace my car. Brian was searching for a vehicle that met all the requirements on my list. He researched different models and ended up choosing a beautiful 10-year-old SUV. The dealer told him that they would inspect the car the following week and that if they found anything wrong beyond preventative maintenance, they would cover it.

Well, they did find something. The left tail light was not working. Seemed like an easy enough fix. However, the previous owner had replaced the original lights with special order LED lights. They planned to charge us for the cost to replace them which would be $300. This was unacceptable to me.

Brian wanted to see if he could replace the lights himself for less money or, if that wasn't possible, through our family mechanic. I kept asking him to take it back to the dealer. It was their responsibility. For some reason he didn't want to do this. I tried not to be pushy and to trust him, but I felt he wasn't holding them to the promise they made when they sold him the car.

Finally, I realized the danger of the situation. I told him that, not only was the left brake light inoperable, but the left turn signal used the same bulb. Brian agreed this was a real danger to me on the highway, with the school commutes, and with my job. He promised to take care of it the following weekend. He rolled his eyes and agreed to call the dealer once more at my request.

The next day I received a text from him saying, "The car dealer doesn't open until 10:00, so I decided to drive to our mechanic to see if they had any advice." He was still intent on going to our family mechanic. I responded, "Ok, thanks." It didn't make any sense to me.

He called me a few minutes later to say that the mechanic had fixed my turn signal. They had a random spare bulb that matched our special order LED light and replaced the malfunctioning bulb without replacing the entire unit. No charge. Not even for labor. I was gently convicted and amazed. God knew. God led him there despite my gentle prodding. It didn't make sense to me, and it *was* the dealer's responsibility, but God took care of it in a different way.

Serve

I have been convicted that I need to be a better servant, not just to my husband, but to my family. The Proverbs 31 Woman has always been an inspiration to me, though her standards seemed too high to obtain. My goodness, this woman is amazing!

"A wife of noble character who can find? She is worth far more than rubies. Her husband has full confidence in her and lacks nothing of value. She brings him good, not harm, all the days of her life." Proverbs 31:10-12

And who can find such a woman? If you read further, you learn that she works hard from dawn until dark, is a great cook, farms, buys and sells, helps the poor, and so much more. I used to look at that passage as a to-do list that I could never check off with my limited time and energy. Recently, while meditating on the passage with a couple friends of mine over breakfast, I began to see it a little differently. This woman serves God as she serves her family. Her reverence for God gives her strength and focus. She fears the Lord and this is her motivation for all her hard work and compassionate acts.

"Charm is deceptive, and beauty is fleeting; but a woman who fears the Lord is to be praised." Proverbs 31:30
I believe she follows the leading of the Holy Spirit. It's not just a checklist. I want this same kind of attitude in serving my own family. I want to allow the Holy Spirit to lead me as I interact with my family. When Brian walks through the door after work, I need to stop what I'm doing and hug him. I need to ask about his day, and not immediately unload on him about mine.

I need to do the mundane things around the house, without complaining, to serve my family. I need to take time for them… listen to my kids and enjoy them. I need to cling to the Holy Spirit when I want to react in anger to the little or big arguments that break out with the kids. I need to deal with each one on a heart level—what are their actions revealing about the status of their hearts? Each day is full of opportunities to show my husband and my children how much I value them, and to teach them Biblical truths. I am on a mission in this home, and outside of it as well. As I serve them I am ultimately serving my God, just like the Proverbs 31 woman. Mother Teresa put it this way:

"All we do— our prayer, our work, our suffering—is for Jesus. Our life has no other reason or motivation… I serve Jesus twenty-four hours a day. Whatever I do is for Him. And He gives me strength. I love Him… He gives us the strength to carry on this life and to do so with happiness." (Conroy, 2016), p.126. I love that!

Savor

While we are not called to be hedonistic in our marriage, seeking our own pleasure and happiness, I believe marriage is meant to be enjoyed. Think about how God presented Eve to Adam in the story of Genesis, as a companion to man. I believe Adam received her from the Lord as a gift, as he exclaimed, *"This is now bone of my bones and flesh of my flesh; she shall be called 'woman,' for she was taken out of man."* The Bible goes on to say, *"For this reason a man will leave his father and mother and be united to his wife, and they will become one flesh. The man and his wife were both naked, and they felt no shame."*

Hello! God included this text for a reason. Jesus referred to the "two becoming one flesh" in both Matthew 19:4-6 and Mark 10:5-9. He didn't mention the naked part, but I believe the writer of Genesis included that detail for a reason. Prior to the Fall of man, Adam and Eve felt no shame in their nakedness. After the Fall, they covered up with fig leaves. Physical union and intimacy in a marriage, let's be honest, feels good, and I believe it is a gift from God as He joins two people together. We should not feel shame over marital intimacy but should embrace it.

We cannot deny that Solomon and his bride, described in the of Song of Solomon, enjoyed one another. In chapter five, the Shulammite woman describes her husband and compliments him from head to toe. In chapter six the groom describes his bride and bestows praise on her. They delight in and enjoy each other. God included this sensuous, poetic book in His living, eternal Word for a reason.

I believe when husbands and wives receive one another as gifts from God, as Adam and Eve did, and enjoy one another with the same mutual fulfillment as Solomon and his bride, being vulnerable and unashamed, we bring honor to God. I bless my husband when I enjoy him and he blesses me when he enjoys me. We both long to be desired. Well, we were made in the image of God, so that makes sense. God wants us to long for Him, to enjoy Him, and to receive the gifts He lavishes upon us. We reflect this giving nature of God when we give to and receive from one another.

I realize it's hard to hear this while still in the dating phase of your relationship. I've asked you to refrain from sexually arousing your sweetie and you are trying to obey the Lord in that. I am very proud of your efforts, by the way.

However, I think it's important to remember that, upon walking down the aisle and saying your vows before God, you have a wonderful gift to unwrap together. It's a gift from God. It's meant to be enjoyed. You can spend the rest of your married life together figuring it out and finding ways to bless one another in ways exclusive to you both. It is worth celebrating.

Brian and I intentionally did not cut corners on our honeymoon. We knew that after the stress leading up to the wedding ceremony, and all the different directions we would be pulled in on the big day, we would need a vacation together. We booked a little cabin in the Poconos in Pennsylvania, complete with a heart shaped tub. The 10-hour road trip gave us time to process everything we had experienced. After 2 years of trying our best to remain pure in our dating, we enjoyed discovering each other all over again. I will spare you the details. It was definitely worth waiting for.

Plan to make sexual intimacy a priority for the health of your relationship. Never hurt one another out of anger or resentment by withholding this gift from one another. Never tease maliciously, but always look for the beauty in this precious act reserved for marriage. Make sure your future spouse always knows you desire him, that you look forward to a sexual life together, and that it will be one of your most important ministries to one another.

There will be times when you won't feel like it. Pray through those times and do what it takes to maintain sexual activity, whether it's getting more sleep, spending more time dating one another or even seeking medical help. Your spouse deserves to be cherished, romanced, and loved and you will be the one to do it. So make it a mission to love your spouse well- physically, spiritually, and emotionally.

Save

Plan to invest in your marriage. It's like a savings account. If you don't add some deposits to your marriage account, there will be nothing to withdraw later. Reading this book together is a wonderful step. But don't stop learning.

Brian and I had the opportunity to host a Couple's Life Group through our church for about 6 years. We wanted to invest in our own marriage while helping other couples who were either engaged or married. We chose various marriage related materials - workbooks, books, or DVD series - and invited other couples to study them with us. Some favorites were Love and Respect by Emerson Eggerichs and Fireproof Your Marriage by Jennifer Dion. We learned so much through those experiences and made some wonderful friends who shared the same goals for their marriages that we do. We gained tools that helped us through rough times and allowed us to keep moving forward in our relationship.

Beyond the life groups, we have invested in our marriage by prioritizing our time together. We guard our nights of intimacy in our home, finding the rhythm that meets both our needs. That's not always easy with small children, but one year for Christmas, I gave Brian a set of door knobs with locks to keep the kids at bay. We go on dates a couple times a month in order to connect. See Chapter 6 for practical ideas.

As our kids grew older this became easier with the support of our family and friends. In the last few years we've added in an overnight getaway, in the dull part of the winter, as a reprieve from the holiday rush. Then we have a little tradition, every five years, of finding a different bed and breakfast for an extended weekend. This allows us to relax and enjoy one another more fully.

Brian is great at surprising me with flowers, especially when I've had a bad day. We leave cards or notes for one another occasionally. He always calls to tell me he's on his way home. We always say, "I love you," when we end phone conversations or part ways. We keep church a priority and always go together. I think the banner hanging over our headboard says it well, "We may not have it all together, but together, we have it all."

I really do feel that way, that I have it all. It may not be Hollywood's version, but thank God for that, right? I have a wonderful God-fearing man to spend the rest of my life with and to raise our children with. I have someone who somehow is still attracted to me after 17 years (22 including dating), and who cherishes me. He forgives me when I mess up and makes me want to be a better wife for him. He makes sure I know that he is striving to be a better husband for me.

Here is a poem I wrote a few years ago:

My Lover and My Friend'

I praise my Lord and my God who
gives me all my needs
Who has led me all along, By His
Spirit gently leads

As I've sought His face, He's been
faithful to advise
He brought my lover and my friend
one who's trustworthy and wise
To walk life's path with me, I know
you were His choice
My heart still leaps within when I
first hear your voice
Your presence fills our home with a peace
that calms my mind
Nowhere in all the world, is a better
one to find.

I thank God for this man and for this marriage. I thank God for loving me so deeply through this person in my life. I pray that by sharing our experiences, including both mistakes and successes, you have gained something of your own. May you honor God in your dating and in every facet of your life. May you always seek God as your first love, and allow that joy and love to spill over into the precious relationships He blesses you with. And may you be a blessing from His hand to those around you.

"And this is my prayer: that your love may abound more and more in knowledge and depth of insight, so that you may be able to discern what is best and may be pure and blameless until the day of Christ, filled with the fruit of righteousness that comes through Jesus Christ—to the glory and praise of God." Philippians 1:9-11

Bibliography

(n.d.). Retrieved November 18, 2016, from Merriam-Webster's Dictionary: www.merriam-webster.com/dictionary/lust

Bell, S. a. (1999). *Made To Be Loved. Enjoying Spiritual Intimacy With God and Your Spouse.* Chicago: Moody Press.

Conroy, Susan (2016). *Praying with Mother Teresa. Prayers, Insights, and Wisdom of Saint Teresa of Calcutta.* Stockbridge: Marian Press.

Chapman, G. (1995). *The Five Love Languages. How to Express Heartfelt Commitment to Your Mate.* Chicago: Northfield Publishing.

DeMoss, N. L. (2001). *Lies Women Believe.* Chicago: Moody Press.

Dion, Jennifer (2008). *Fireproof Your Marriage Participant's Guide 2nd Edition.* Vista, CA: Outreach Publishing.

Dr. Emerson Eggerichs (2016). *Love and Respect Live Conference and 10 Week Study.* Grand Rapids, Michigan: Love and Respect Ministries.

Dr. Les Parrott, D. L. (2015). *Saving Your Marriage Before It Starts. Seven Questions to Ask Before—and After—You Marry.* Zondervan.

Hybels, B. a. (1993). *Fit To Be Tied. Making Marriage Last A Lifetime.* Grand Rapids, Michigan: Zondervan.

International Service Organization of SAA, I. (2007-2016). *Sexaholics Anonymous.* Retrieved November 25, 2016, from Sex Addicts Anonymous: https://saa-recovery.org

Kendall, D. J. (1995). *Lady In Waiting.* Shippensburg, PA: Treasure House.

Moore, B. (2000). *Breaking Free: Making Liberty in Christ a Reality In Life.* Nashville: Briadman & Holman Publishers.

Sherman, D. (1999). *Love, Sex and Relationships.* Seattle, Washington: Youth With a Mission.

Trace, A. (2008). *Cohabitation as a Means to Marriage.* Retrieved November 25, 2016, from Focus On The Family, Helping Families Thrive: www.focusonthefamily.com/ marriage/preparing-for-marriage/test-driving-marriage/ cohabitation-as-a-means-of-marriage

Trent C. Butler, P. (1991). *Holman Bible Dictionary.* Nashville,TN: Holman Bible Publishers.

Bible References taken from the New International Version

About the Author

L aura Mayer is a wife and mother, Occupational Therapist and speaker. She has been involved in multiple women's and children's ministries since 2001. She and her husband, Brian, have been married 17 years and live in Indianapolis, Indiana with their three children. She shares her journey as she came to know Jesus through her life experiences in her relationships as well as through her recovery from an eating disorder.

Note from Brian

The details contained in this book regarding me may be unflattering, but at no time are they inaccurate. It is true that I have struggled with pornography and lust, and no amount of gloss or spin can negate that reality. It is a large part of the reason why I begin my testimony with the statement "My story has a happy ending, but that doesn't make it a happy story."

I didn't know God's plan for my life and marriage as being the best and most fulfilling path I could choose to travel. I do now, and one of my greatest regrets is realizing how much deeper my connection could have been, both between God and my wife, if I had accepted that truth earlier. Regardless of that, the fact remains that God has chosen to forgive me of my past and cover me with His grace. The pursuit of reclaiming the purity that I took from both of us was a road that I didn't fully appreciate (or even understand) while I was travelling on it, but as I look back now I see the value and it makes me appreciate my wife, as well her heart for those that are willing to struggle and strive for God-honoring relationships.

His ways are not our ways; purity fights against not only culture, but biology and man's sinful nature. It is a spiritual battle fought daily through flesh, and losses will happen. However, because of God and His grace we are not defined by our failures, but His triumph (2Cor 4:16)! From one who has been where you are, let me speak to those who may be wary or even uninterested in the hard truths therein: your boyfriend or girlfriend is absolutely worth YOUR pursuit of purity! Choosing the path of purity demonstrates that you are willing to treat them with the same value and care that God does. Even if you don't see the value in it now that is okay, because you are trading physical benefits now for greater spiritual benefits later! It is perfectly acceptable to begin walking the road to purity because God commands you to, and over time I pray that He will open your eyes and your heart, so you will one day do it because He loves you and wants only the best for you. Remember that it brings God tremendous joy when we choose to follow His commands.

Reclaiming Purity: A Couple's Study Guide

Your Journey to Live God's Way in a Christian Dating Relationship, and in Marriage

LAURA C. MAYER

Early Notions
Read Chapters 1-2.

1. Name a couple of movies that contributed to your ideas of dating. How do you think they influenced you?

Him:_____

_____

_____

Her:_____

_____

_____

2. Who in your life shaped your expectations of dating? What ideas did you get from those people?

Him:_____

_____

_____

Her:_____

_____

_____

3. How has the culture impacted your ideas on body image? Do you have any expectations of your partner to look a certain way?

Him:_____

_____

_____

Her:_____

_____

_____

4. Have you allowed the desire to look a certain way or attract the opposite sex become more important in your life than God? What have you been striving for?

Him:_____

_____

_____

Her:_____

_____

_____

5. What first attracted you to your partner and stirred your heart?

Him:_____

_____

_____

Her:_____

_____

_____

6. Describe your first date together.

Him:_____

_____

_____

Her:_____

_____

_____

7. How did your partner make you feel on that first date?

Him:_____

_____

_____

Her:_____

_____

_____

8. Have you ever taken some steps too far in your dating relationships? How did you rationalize it at the time?

Him:_____

_____

_____

Her:_____

_____

_____

9. What was the damage to your walk with God and relationships as a result of those choices?

Him:_____

_____

_____

Her:_____

_____

_____

10. Looking back on those experiences, how would you have done things differently?

Him:_____

_____

_____

Her:_____

_____

_____

Spend some time in prayer, seeking God's wisdom in the area of dating, and repenting of any past mistakes. Allow God to cleanse you of any idols related to body image. Receive God's forgiveness as you walk a new path to honor Him.

Come to Jesus
Read Chapter 3

1. What has your church experience been like thus far?

Him:_____

_____

_____

Her:_____

_____

_____

2. Who in your life has shaped your view of God and Jesus? Is that view in line with what the Bible says about God?

Him:_____

_____

_____

Her:_____

_____

_____

3. Have you had a "come to Jesus moment"? What brought you to your knees?

Him:_____

_____

_____

Her:_____

_____

_____

4. In what ways do you notice your need for Jesus today?

Him:_____

_____

_____

Her:_____

_____

_____

5. What do you look for in a church? What's important to you
    when it comes to worship?

Him:_____

_____

_____

Her:_____

_____

_____

6. Have you had to give your partner space in his or her walk
    with God? In what ways?

Him:_____

_____

_____

Her:_____

_____

_____

7. What do you most appreciate in your partner's walk with God?

Him:_____

_____

_____

Her:_____

_____

_____

8. How are you and your partner encouraging one another today in your walks with Jesus?

Him:_____

_____

_____

Her:_____

_____

_____

9. What lessons would you want any future children of yours (or nieces or nephews) to learn from your walk with God so far?

Him:_____

_____

_____

Her:_____

_____

_____

10. As you pray about your partner, what do you sense God is speaking over him or her?

Him:_____

_____

_____

Her:_____

_____

_____

Spend some time in prayer right now, speaking loving words over your partner and seeking God's guidance for your relationship. Thank Him for your own "Come to Jesus" moment.

Play by the Rules
Read Chapter 4

1. How important is the idea of purity in a dating relationship to you and why?

Him:_____

_____

_____

Her:_____

_____

_____

2. What rules of the 21st century are in conflict with how God has asked us to live?

Him:_____

_____

_____

Her:_____

_____

_____

3. Can you give an example, either from your own life or from someone you have observed, of how someone's "house built on sand" came crashing down in a storm?

Him:_____

_____

_____

Her:_____

_____

_____

4. How might you have been guilty of "playing house" either in your current relationship or in a past dating relationship? What were some of the negative consequences?

Him:_____

_____

_____

Her:_____

_____

_____

5. Why do you think Jesus referred to the Genesis passage when He was talking to His hearers about marriage?

Him:_____

_____

_____

Her:_____

_____

_____

6. Have you had difficulty accepting the Bible's teaching on submission regarding marriage in Ephesians chapter 5? Have you seen submission modeled well in other people's marriages? Give an example.

Him:_____

_____

_____

Her:_____

_____

_____

7. Where have you seen the idea of submission misconstrued?

Him:_____

_____

_____

Her:_____

_____

_____

8. What do you feel God maybe teaching your heart today about His concept of submission in marriage?

Him:_____

_____

_____

Her:_____

_____

_____

9. Do you see any obstacles in your ability to leave your parents and cleave to your spouse? Why is this so important for unity within a marriage?

Him:_____

_____

_____

Her:_____

_____

_____

10. What can you do to walk in His blessing in regard to your future marriage relationship?

Him:_____

_____

_____

Her:_____

_____

_____

11. How does the concept of modesty impact you? What changes do you need to make in your own dress or the way

you carry yourself? (or how you respond to others' dress or attitudes)

Him:_____

_____

_____

Her:_____

_____

_____

12. Why is it so important to draw a line in our physical boundaries?

Him:_____

_____

_____

Her:_____

_____

_____

13. What line do you feel God wants you to draw in your physical boundaries with dating? Name specific physical activities that would push you into that realm of temptation.

Him:_____

_____

_____

Her:_____
_____
_____

14. How can we avert your focus from what you are missing out
on in your physical relationship?

Him:_____
_____
_____

Her:_____
_____
_____

15. Have you had any accountability partners in the past, either
regarding this issue or with another area of struggle? How
was it helpful to guard you from temptation?

Him:_____
_____
_____

Her:_____
_____
_____

16. Who will you be accountable to for keeping that boundary line in your dating? How often will you contact him/her?

Him:_____

_____

_____

Her:_____

_____

_____

Pray together, praising God for His beautiful design in marriage, confess ways that each of you have fallen short of protecting the sanctity of your future marriage relationships, and vow to begin following God's guidelines to honor Him.

Placing God in the Center
Read Chapter 5

1. Have you struggled with legalism, following the rules out of a sense of duty or trying to earn God's love? How has that looked in your own life?

Him:_____

_____

_____

Her:_____

_____

_____

2. In your own words, what is the purpose of the Law, or God's rules for us?

Him:_____

_____

_____

Her:_____

_____

_____

3. Do you believe and accept the fact that through Jesus' work for you on the cross, you have His righteousness? What does that mean in light of obedience to God?

Him:_____

_____

_____

Her:_____

_____

_____

4. Read John 14:15-26. What does Jesus say about obedience?
   What has God given to us to help us follow Him?

Him:_____

_____

_____

Her:_____

_____

_____

5. Do you currently have a habit of "Quiet times" with Jesus?
   What does that look like and how has it changed over the
   years?

Him:_____

_____

_____

Her:_____

_____

_____

6. How have you grown in your prayer life? Where do you need to grow still? For example, are you going to God at all for your needs, learning to rely on Him and trust Him day to day? Next, have you been able to go beyond your needs in prayer, to ask what God might want of *you* to further His kingdom? How can you begin to move outwardly to bless others in prayer?

Him:_____
_____
_____

Her:_____
_____
_____

7. Has God ever used nature or an object as a lesson for you? (Like the flag waving in the wind) How has that helped you to embrace a Biblical truth?

Him:_____
_____
_____

Her:_____
_____
_____

8. Read through the list from my journal on page 48 about tangible steps to solidify a love life with the Lord. Circle or

write down three to five that stand out to you that can help you in your walk with Jesus.

Him:_____

_____

_____

Her:_____

_____

_____

9. How do you see the Holy Spirit currently present in your dating relationship and creating a cord of three strands?

Him:_____

_____

_____

Her:_____

_____

_____

10. What is something that you as a couple can begin that would strengthen that cord, and further help you as a couple to remain in the Vine that Jesus described in John 15?

Him:_____

_____

_____

Her:_____

_____

_____

11. Have you experienced the Holy Spirit guiding you in a
decision you've made in the past, personally or as a couple?
How did He make His will known to you?

Him:_____

_____

_____

Her:_____

_____

_____

12. Think of a decision that you are facing together as a couple
today. Write out how you can submit that decision to God
by asking for guidance from the Holy Spirit.

Him:_____

_____

_____

Her:_____

_____

_____

Spend some time praying together, possibly confessing for times when you have not allowed the Holy Spirit to be part of your lives and relationships (even unawares) and inviting God to be intertwined in your lives moving forward. What areas of your relationship do you need to submit to God?

What do we do with ourselves?
Read Chapter 6

1. Can you relate to my statement that our relationship had
   been reduced to a purely physical one? How has that looked
   for you?

Him:_____

_____

_____

Her:_____

_____

_____

2. What old patterns of dating have you been tempted to fall
   back into?

Him:_____

_____

_____

Her:_____

_____

_____

3. Do you have a firm boundary of what you will or will not
   do physically together? What is that boundary?

Him:_____

_____

_____

Her:_____

_____

_____

4. Who are you accountable to for sticking to that boundary?
   How will you contact that accountability partner each time
   you and your partner have a date?

Him:_____

_____

_____

Her:_____

_____

_____

5. Which two budget dates would you like to try?

Him:_____

_____

_____

Her:_____

_____

_____

6. What benefits to your relationship do you see in thinking of group dates?

Him:_____

_____

_____

Her:_____

_____

_____

7. Who could you go out on a group date with and what could you do together?

Him:_____

_____

_____

Her:_____

_____

_____

8. What kingdom purposes are heavy on your heart?

Him:_____

_____

_____

Her:_____

_____

9. Are you aware of your own gifts that God has created you with? (see 1Cor 12-14 and…)

Him:_____

_____

_____

Her:_____

_____

_____

10. What can you do to invest in those kingdom purposes together on a date?

Him:_____

_____

_____

Her:_____

_____

_____

11. What is your favorite "Alone in a Crowd" date that you and your partner have had in the past?

Him:_____

_____

_____

Her:_____

_____

_____

12. Which "Alone in a Crowd" date would you like to try?

Him:_____

_____

_____

Her:_____

_____

_____

13. What similarities and differences do these lists of date ideas bring about between you and your dating partner? What kinds of things do you both enjoy doing? How do your preferences differ? What can you do about those differences? (For instance, if I love going to the state fair but he doesn't, does he make a sacrifice once in a while to do this with me, or do I simply do those kinds of activities with my mom and girlfriends instead?)

Him:_____

_____

_____

Her:_____

14. Are you familiar with Gary Chapman's <u>Five Love Languages?</u> Do you have any idea what your primary love language would be (Words of Affirmation, Works of Service, Physical touch, Quality Time, Gifts?) Share together what your impression is and if you don't know, I recommend checking out that book.

Him:_____

_____

_____

Her:_____

_____

_____

15. Have you ever tried to show love to a person in your life through your own love language that maybe wasn't the same as theirs?

Him:_____

_____

_____

Her:_____

_____

_____

16. How can you move beyond your own comfort zone to show someone (maybe your partner) love in a language that is not your strongest but is meaningful for them?

Him:_____
_____
_____

Her:_____
_____
_____

Pray together that God would bless your dating relationship, giving you creative ways to invest in one another, that would honor Him. Then plan your next date.

Purity After a Broken Marriage or Relationship
Read Chapter 7

1. What relationships have you each experienced in your past that failed? Can you identify what caused them to dissolve? (offenses adding up, unmet expectations, infidelity, lack of connection or communication?)

Him:_____

_____

_____

Her:_____

_____

_____

2. What things did you try to save those relationships?

Him:_____

_____

_____

Her:_____

_____

_____

3. Do you feel that you are at times guarded emotionally in your current relationship because of past hurts? How does this show up in your interactions?

Him:_____

_____

_____

Her:_____

_____

_____

4. What steps have you taken to prevent some of the same pitfalls in your current relationship?

Him:_____

_____

_____

Her:_____

_____

_____

5. Have you sought counseling for some of the hurts in your past? How might this contribute to the health of your current relationship?

Him:_____

_____

_____

Her:_____

_____

_____

6. Try to think of at least 2 unspoken expectations that you may be placing on your current partner. Discuss if these are expectations that you each can agree to or find a compromise in some way. (could be as simple as "I feel like you should call me on your way home from work", or as large as how many children you hope to have.)

Him:_____

_____

_____

Her:_____

_____

_____

7. Find a scripture verse that can help you to let go of offenses moving forward. Commit to memorize it.

Him:_____

_____

_____

Her:_____

_____

_____

8. What are 2 things you can do to protect your current relationship from infidelity?

Him:_____

_____

_____

Her:_____

_____

_____

9. What is your favorite way to connect with your partner? (For
    example, I like to catch up with Brian as we walk the dog
    at night.) What can you do to ensure that each of you has
    their needs met for connection in a way that is meaningful?

Him:_____

_____

_____

Her:_____

_____

_____

10. If you have been married or sexually active with past
    relationships, what can you do today to guard your purity?

Him:_____

_____

_____

Her:_____

_____

_____

Read Isaiah 61:1-11 together. Take turns praying over one another, that God would comfort his/her broken heart, free them from any chains (break any emotional ties to past partners), give them a beautiful crown to replace the ashes, replace their sorrow with joy, replace a spirit of sadness with a spirit of praise. Pray that God would rebuild the places that were destroyed in your partner's life, and that they will enjoy His blessings through a covenant with God.

Engagement
Read Chapter 8

1. If you are engaged, how did you (or he) pop the question? And what was your favorite part of the evening?

Him:_____
_____
_____

Her:_____
_____
_____

2. If you aren't engaged, what are the things that you still would like to learn about your partner before that season begins?

Him:_____
_____
_____

Her:_____
_____
_____

3. How do you think being engaged will change or impact your current relationship? Think of challenges as well as joys.

Him:_____

_____

_____

Her:_____

_____

_____

4. Have you tried to be the mediator between God and your partner? Are there any ways that you need to step down? Or step up? (in reference to being the spiritual leader of the relationship)

Him:_____

_____

_____

Her:_____

_____

_____

5. Have the two of you ever experienced geographical distance in your relationship? How did it challenge you? How did God use this season to grow your relationship?

Him:_____

_____

_____

Her:_____

6. Can you relate to the temptation to rationalize giving into physical temptations once being engaged? (read paragraph 3 on pg 81) How can you press into your commitment to your First Love to remain pure?

Him:_____

_____

_____

Her:_____

_____

_____

7. What are some words of affirmation you can give to your partner to verbally assure him or her that they are the only one for you, since you are limited with your physical affection?

Him:_____

_____

_____

Her:_____

_____

_____

8. What elements of your story, your personalities and your faith would you like to involve in your wedding ceremony? Can you think of ways to do this through songs, traditions, or favors?

Him:_____

_____

_____

Her:_____

_____

_____

9. What little foxes are threatening to ruin your vineyard? (Song of Sol. 2:14-15) In other words, what troubles are you experiencing in your relationship: annoyances, differences, or grievances? Can you think of ways to resolve these grievances? Are there some that you feel God is asking you to simply overlook? Psalm 19:11 says "A person's wisdom yields patience; it is to one's glory to overlook an offense."

Him:_____

_____

_____

Her:_____

_____

_____

10. What are some ways God is calling you to give grace to your partner?

Him:_____

_____

_____

Her:_____

_____

_____

11. What steps can you take during this season of engagement to make sure that you not only plan for a special wedding day and honeymoon, but that you plan for a successful marriage as well?

Him:_____

_____

_____

Her:_____

_____

_____

Pray that God would continue to guide you both in this relationship, that it would bring glory and honor to His name, and that through it He would make you both more into the image of His Son Jesus as you learn to celebrate one another, love one another, guard one another, and give each other grace and forgiveness. May He prepare you for what's ahead in His will for you as you ponder marriage.

Rocky Roads
Read Chapter 9

1. What are your goals for your future? This can relate to your jobs, your location, your areas of ministry, children and even pets.

Him:_____

_____

_____

Her:_____

_____

_____

2. What's the biggest dream in your heart?

Him:_____

_____

_____

Her:_____

_____

_____

3. Are these dreams and goals in line with your future spouse? Would either of you have to sacrifice anything when you come together in marriage?

Him:_____

Her:_____

_____

_____

4. Have you ever tested your partner as I did with Brian, to see if he or she was truly committed to you?

Him:_____

_____

_____

Her:_____

_____

_____

5. Was there a time when you held back your true feelings because you were afraid of how your partner would take it? (Like Brian who agreed to our break-up because he thought that's what I wanted.)

Him:_____

_____

_____

Her:_____

_____

_____

6. What are your areas of insecurity? Are you fearful that you won't be pretty enough? Are you afraid you won't make enough money or get the right job? Are you insecure of what your future in-laws will think of you? Are you afraid your spouse will fall out of love with you?

Him:_____

_____

_____

Her:_____

_____

_____

7. Have you truly made Jesus your First Love so that your security can lie in Him and how He sees you? Can you trust in Him to provide for you everything that you need for the vocations He is calling you to?

Him:_____

_____

_____

Her:_____

_____

_____

8. How can you show the world the love and grace of God through your current relationships and circumstances?

Him:_____

_____

_____

Her:_____

_____

_____

9. Can you make a commitment to your partner to accept the
    "much grace required" state of marriage? Will you commit
    to ongoing maintenance in this relationship so that you
    will continue to be refined and conformed into the image
    of Christ and His Church? What might that maintenance
    look like?

Him:_____

_____

_____

Her:_____

_____

_____

10. How have you expected your partner to read your mind
    during the years you've been together?

Him:_____

_____

_____

Her:_____

_____

_____

11. Is there an area that you have expected perfection from your partner that God is asking you to let go of?

Him:_____

_____

_____

Her:_____

_____

_____

12. Do you see in your partner a heart of submission to Christ? Do you see an attitude of being willing to make adjustments and to give grace? Do you have this same attitude?

Him:_____

_____

_____

Her:_____

_____

_____

13. How has God shown you His own immense love for you? (cite Scripture if you can). Can you trust Him with your future dreams and your future relationships?

Him:_____

_____

_____

Her:_____

_____

_____

Confess to one another where you have expected too much, tested one another's commitment, lied about your feelings or refused to forgive. Vow to make a commitment to one another, to submit first and foremost to God, and to be faithful to one another, to honor your future marriage above all other relationships and to do what it takes to grow in love and grace regardless of feelings and what's deserved. Pray for God to give you strength through the Holy Spirit to walk in His ways to be the best imitator of Christ that you can be.

Replacing the Shame and Guilt
Read Chapter 10

1. Have you ever been caught in the act of a sinful behavior? Did you experience accusations like the woman in John 8, or did someone give you grace?

Him:_____

_____

_____

Her:_____

_____

_____

2. How have you been the one holding the stone?

Him:_____

_____

_____

Her:_____

_____

_____

3. Tell about a time you had the opportunity to give someone else grace.

Him:_____

_____

Her:_____

_____

_____

4. Do you truly believe God has forgiven your sins, past present and future through Jesus' sacrifice on the cross? How is this played out in your life? (Are you still carrying around the shame or are you able to worship God out of thankfulness for His grace?)

Him:_____

_____

_____

Her:_____

_____

_____

5. When your own sin has been exposed, have you responded by rationalizing it, denying it, or giving excuses?

Him:_____

_____

_____

Her:_____

_____

_____

6. Do you sense any walls in your relationship with your Heavenly Father? What can you surrender to Him today?

Him:_____

_____

_____

Her:_____

_____

_____

7. The woman in John 8 was found to be guilty, but her accusers were found to be no less guilty. In Christ she was given a choice. Jesus no longer condemned her but He did call her to a higher standard. Have you been given a turning point? Have you made the choice to turn away from a destructive path and choose a redeemed life in Christ, walking in freedom? Explain.

Him:_____

_____

_____

Her:_____

_____

_____

8. Have you tried to change in your own efforts, possibly with rules and regulations? How is that working for you?

Him:_____

_____

_____

Her:_____

_____

_____

9. What sinful patterns of the past have become less alluring for you as you have made room for the Holy Spirit in your life?

Him:_____

_____

_____

Her:_____

_____

_____

10. Read Isaiah 43:18-19. How has Jesus made a way in the wilderness for you? What new things is He doing in your life and heart?

Him:_____

_____

_____

Her:_____

_____

_____

11. What can you do to focus on the new creation and forget the former things of the past?

Him:_____

_____

_____

Her:_____

_____

_____

12. If you are to live your life out, forever indebted to Jesus for His unending forgiveness and grace, what would that look like? Can you relate to the woman who broke her jar at His feet in worship?

Him:_____

_____

_____

Her:_____

_____

_____

13. How is Jesus tugging on your heart in regard to forgiving others for their grievances against you?

Him:_____

_____

_____

Her:_____

_____

_____

Spend some time voicing your love and forgiveness for your partner for anything you may have been holding against him or her. Confess your own grievances towards your partner. Pray together, thanking God for sending His son to die in your place on the cross, and for refusing to condemn you as your sins deserved. Vow to serve Him all your days and to extend the same love, grace and forgiveness to your partner as well as to others in your lives.

Moving from Hedonism to Godliness
Read Chapter 11

1. Have you been guilty of placing "Happily Ever After" as the goal for your future?

Him:_____

_____

_____

Her:_____

_____

_____

2. How have you changed in your walk with Christ to begin living for His will and His glory instead of just your own happiness? How have you seen this in your partner?

Him:_____

_____

_____

Her:_____

_____

_____

3. Read 1 Corinthians 13:4-8. As I describe this heavenly love on pages 108-109, where are you challenged the most?

Him:_____

Her:_____

_____

_____

4. How are you being challenged to show sacrificial love and respect for your partner as described in Ephesians 5?

Him:_____

_____

_____

Her:_____

_____

_____

5. How can the two of you shift your thinking to move towards one another in unity? What desires can you set aside in order to bless one another and move through conflict?

Him:_____

_____

_____

Her:_____

_____

_____

6. How can each of you submit to God in your relationship? If you are the woman, can you accept your calling to submit to your husband out of reverence for God?

Him:_____

_____

_____

Her:_____

_____

_____

7. How do you sense God calling you to serve in all your spheres of influence? Do you feel the impact this makes on the sense of meaning in your life?

Him:_____

_____

_____

Her:_____

_____

_____

8. If you are engaged to be married and are looking towards a date for your wedding, describe how you intend to savor your physical relationship once you are married. Here's some advice: you each can keep a journal, and whenever you are tempted to cross your boundaries while dating, instead of acting on those impulses, write some thoughts

in the journal. This can be a sweet and sensuous gift you exchange on your honeymoon. It can be an outlet for those feelings rather than stifling them.

Him:_____

_____

_____

Her:_____

_____

_____

9. What would you like to plan for your honeymoon? Where would you like to go? What activities would you like to do (outside the room). What are some of your expectations for inside the room? Vow to adjust your expectations so that both partners are ministered to.

Him:_____

_____

_____

Her:_____

_____

_____

10. If you make it your mission to love your future spouse well, physically, spiritually and emotionally, can you speak to each of these areas? What's a way you can fulfill this mission?

Him:_____

_____

_____

Her:_____

_____

_____

11. What investments do you anticipate making in your future
    marriage over the years?

Him:_____

_____

_____

Her:_____

_____

_____

Read Philippians 1:9-11 together. Pray that God gives you both
the discernment you need to walk in His ways, to keep learning
more of Him, more of one another and to have the strength
to love and minister to one another well both now and in the
future. Pray that your relationship would bring glory and honor
to His Name and would draw others to His wonderful family as
they are attracted to your love and grace for one another.

Be blessed! Wouldn't it be fun if you could post your picture
on my facebook page at

https://www.facebook.com/Laura-C-Mayer-477975406
343211/?modal=admin_todo_tour

Printed in the United States
By Bookmasters

.